71 Fu

MW01268536

71 Fun Ways to Make Life Easier

Energy, Meditation, and Relaxation Techniques for Everyone

Judy May

2008

Copyright © 2008 Judy May
All rights reserved.
ISBN: 1-4196-9079-5
ISBN-13: 978-1419690792

71 Fun Ways to Make Life Easier

Dedicated to
Lee Harrington
Thank you for your help and support.

✌

Also dedicated to you, the reader.

✌

I've used these techniques for years.
They will make a big difference in how you will feel on a daily basis.

✌

Use them in good health!

Table of Contents

INTRODUCTION

A HAPPIER YOU

The following 71 techniques are all about your body's energy and working with the universal energies. They will teach you how to maintain your energy so that you will feel balanced on a daily basis. You may already be aware of how your energy gets mixed with the energy of others and theirs with yours. But you probably don't know that you can separate these energies, let alone, how to separate them.

You are bombarded with other people's energy every day. Whether you are at work, church, shopping, at home with the kids, with your friends, out to eat or anywhere there is a gathering of people. Sometimes you might meet up with just one person and the amount of energy that is exchanged can wear you out. You might not even be aware that their energy can affect you. It does, and the results can vary from being more tired than usual or necessary; feeling depressed or angry and not knowing why; even to hearing someone arguing with you in your mind. These are just a few of the negative ways others energy can affect you.

At the same time you are picking up others energy, you are also giving away your own. When you give your energy away, be it to your children, partner or anyone you're around, you will feel tired. You can compare your giving away energy to a tire that slowly goes flat. You don't realize the tire is losing air until it is finally flat. In the same way, you don't realize you are giving away your energy until you run out and feel tired. When you give away your energy and take on someone else's, that doesn't match your own, you will find it difficult to function. Your thoughts and feelings become jumbled and you may make decisions you wouldn't have made if you'd felt balanced and clear.

When you are carrying others energy in your body it's hard to know how you are feeling. It's sometimes difficult to understand why you may have reacted to someone in a certain way. You might be reacting in a negative way because you just spoke to someone who was angry and they threw that anger at you. You are carrying that anger with you and are now throwing it at someone else. It's just like throwing a baseball. You throw it, someone catches it. The throwing and catching happens all day long. Is it any wonder that you're so tired at the end of the day? By releasing other's energy and reclaiming your own, you will have more energy through out the day. It's important that after you've exchanged energy with others you regain your balance. When you are balanced you will be able to experience others and your environment with more awareness and joy.

Other techniques are described that will help you work with the universal energies. They are fun. They will help clear your environment, relax, protect yourself and even help you in finding a parking space. These techniques will help you make use of your own ability to create a more enjoyable reality. I've found the processes very useful for others as well as myself. I know they'll work for you regardless of your age or background. You'll soon learn about the many ways in which energy, in its diversity of forms, affects how you experience life. I hope you'll find both enjoyment and practical benefit in the following pages.

Note

In many of the techniques I suggest pushing the negative energy into the earth. Because Mother Earth is so polluted and saturated with chemicals and such, when possible place the negative energy into an imaginary fire to burn and transmute. Some of the imagery makes it difficult to transmute in a fire, so if it's easier have the energy go into the earth. Use your judgment with each technique.

Managing Your Energy

The easiest way to understand energy is to compare it to electricity. Electricity comes from an outside force such as water or wind. In order for you to use the electricity, it must run through power lines into your home. The electricity flows throughout your home through wires. You can access that electricity through outlets. If you overload an outlet you will blow a circuit, cutting off the flow of electricity. You have energy flowing throughout your body in much the same way. Just as with electricity, if you get overloaded, you will blow a circuit. That's why it's important to manage your energy.

Energy not only moves through your body but through all living things throughout the universe. This energy vibrates in each body and everything at different levels. Because everyone's energy runs at a different vibration they do not blend. It's like trying to blend water and oil. No matter how hard you try they will not blend. And just like water and oil remain separated, you need to separate your energy from others.

To ensure a good session with my clients I make sure they clear their energy before we begin working. It's important that they are working within their own energy system. If they came from work they need to eliminate the work environment's energy. I don't want the confusion or personalities from work to interfere with our session. I ask clients to take a moment to get centered and bring all of their energy back to themselves with the techniques you will learn in this book. When they are no longer distracted by the energy of others, we begin. They feel more relaxed and centered and it allows our session to be more productive.

Letting go of the energy of others leads to better management of your own energy and a healthier, happier you. The more attune you become to your energy, the higher your vibration level will be. This enables you to feel a stronger connection to the outside universal energy that connects us all. When you work with the universal energy you will find it easier to heal yourself and be more aware of the changes coming into your life. Instead of panicking because unexpected things are happening at work, you'll see these happenings as a sign from the universe that something is about to change in your life. You will flow with the change instead of being stressed about it. Allow the energy to flow through you and manage it through clearing out the negative energies.

Here's a simple way to discover how much energy you can feel:

Hold your hands with palms facing each other approximately five inches apart. Move your hands away from each other several inches then slowly bring them back towards each other. Repeat this process several times. Do your hands or fingers tingle, feel warm, feel pressure or have any other sensation? Everyone feels energy differently so go with your feelings. If your hands feel warm then that's how you feel energy.

Another way to feel energy is to have a friend hold their hands with palms facing each other approximately five inches apart. Use either your finger or entire hand and slowly move them between your friend's palms. Can you feel anything? You might feel a tingling sensation, pressure or warmth. If you don't feel anything then try this with other friends. Some individuals don't emit enough energy through their hands for you to feel. So it might not be that you can't feel the energy, it might be that they don't emit enough energy to be felt.

Don't worry if you can't feel energy or if you only feel a small amount. The more you work with energy the easier it will be to feel. Eventually, you will begin to feel energy shifts within your body and your environment. The more energy you feel the more you will need to manage that energy to ensure your comfort.

Learning to Visualize

Throughout this book you will be asked to "visualize" or "imagine" certain things. Visualizing happens when you allow your mind to see images or pictures without having to force it. This may or may not be easy for you. If someone says imagine yourself in a beautiful place by the ocean. Can you immediately see yourself sitting on the beach by the ocean or do you struggle to conjure up that image? It's great if imagining or visualizing is easy for you. Use that method of visualizing.

On the other hand if this is difficult then you need to try a different approach. If you can't "see" a clear image, you may "feel" it instead. That is, you might feel the sand under your feet and a spray of water. This means you "feel" instead of "see". Feeling works just as well as seeing when you need to visualize or imagine. Trust whatever process works for you. Neither is correct nor incorrect because everyone receives information differently.

If you can see and feel, that's fabulous, but don't get caught up in what you can and cannot do. Your unique abilities will get you the information you need. Make a mental note of the form you use to visualize and allow that to be your frame of reference for all visualizations.

Chapter 1

ENERGY AND YOUR BODY

Chakras

Chakras are powerful energy centers within the body that branch from the human nervous system. The word chakra literally translates as wheel or disk. These wheels or disks are spinning spheres. Chakras receive, assimilate and express life form energy. Each chakra vibrates at a different frequency and has a different symbol, color and sound. To function properly each chakra needs to be balanced, clear, properly spinning and at its correct frequency.

There are seven major chakras in the trunk of the body and four secondary chakras in the hands and feet. There are eight minor chakras that are mentioned as reference only. The major chakras deal with your emotions and your spirituality. The secondary have to do with action and physicality.

Seven Major Chakras

The locations and generally accepted meanings of the Major Chakras are as follows: (Others refer to the third chakra as being located approximately two inches above the naval. I find the naval itself a more powerful energy spot.)

1.	Tail bone (root)	Survival, support, right to exist
2.	Above the pubic bone	Sexuality, creativity, right to feel

3.	Naval	Power center, right to act
4.	Heart	Love, compassion, right to love- be loved
5.	Throat	Communication, right to speak and hear
6.	Middle of Forehead (3rd eye)	Clear seeing
7.	Top of Head (crown)	Spiritual knowledge, knowingness
8.	Above Head, three inches	Soul, brings in spirit energy

As you can see I have made reference to the eighth chakra. I feel the eighth chakra is important, as it is your soul chakra. As you work with energy you will become more connected to your soul. This connection is imperative to living as a spiritual being.

The chakras are wheels or disks that spin. So, to help you visualize the energy of the major chakras (2nd through 6th), imagine a tunnel with wind swirling rapidly through it that goes through the body from back to the front. Energy is spinning through the tunnel (chakra) at a high speed. You can open the chakra as wide as you want; the more open the chakra, the more energy is flowing through your body. But, you can, so to speak, blow your circuits! That is why it's best to have the chakras remain open only about a quarter of an inch. The 1st and 7th chakras are shaped like a funnel. The root chakra funnel begins at the tailbone and expands downward; the crown funnel begins at the top of the head and opens upwards.

Thus, your energy flow enters through the funnel at the top of your head, the crown chakra (7th), descends through the 6th chakra, continues toward the 5th to the 2nd chakra, and flows out through the 1st chakra into the ground.

Four Secondary Chakras

Two chakras are located on the hands, one in the middle of each palm.

These are the creative healing chakras. You will use these

chakras often. The other two, in the middle of the soles of the feet, are used to help you ground or center your body to the physical world.

Eight Minor Chakras

I mention these chakras in Aligning the Body and Chakra Opening Meditation. It is good to refer to them when you have physical ailments located in these chakras area. For example if your elbow is bothering you are having an issue with being flexible. You might be having an argument with someone and you are not being flexible in your opinions. (Refer to *You Can Heal Your Life* by Louise L. Hay on physical ailments. I have found that Louise is pretty right on when associating ailments to issues. She describes the elbows dealing with movement of direction and knees having to deal with flexibility. It's important that you use what feels right for you.) You will also find these chakras referred to as meridians in Chinese healing.

Eight Minor Chakras:

• Knees (2)	Movement
• Elbow (2)	Flexibility
• Thigh (2)	Stability
• Shoulders	Strength
• Genitalia	Reproduction

You can learn more about chakras on the Internet, at your local library or through books by other authors. Here are a few books on Chakras: *Chakras for Beginners* by David Pond; *The Chakra Bible* by Patricia Mercier; *The Book of Chakras* by Ambika Wauters; *Your Aura and Your Chakras* by Karla McLaren.

Meridians

Meridians are acupressure vessels located throughout the body. They actually contain a free-flowing, colorless, non-cellular liquid. Modern technology methods have actually

measured and mapped meridians. Along each meridian there
are specific acupuncture points, which are electro-magnetic in
character. There are well over five hundred points in the body.
The Chinese physicians have used meridians to detect illnesses
for centuries. By feeling specific acupuncture points they can
detect imbalances within the body. Often these imbalances are
caused by the stress in your life. A break in the flow of energy
can be compared to overloading circuits or popping a circuit
breaker. When the flow of energy is interrupted, the flow needs
resetting.

Do you ever have a feeling of being out-of-balance? Are
you wired, as if you'd had twenty cups of coffee? Do you feel
like you're going to faint or like you can't calm down enough
to sleep? When that out-of-balance sensation overtakes you,
there are some simple techniques that can help restore your
equilibrium. You can use these techniques on yourself, your
mate, your children, friends, or even pets.

Resetting the Flow

The following meridian balancing processes are easy to
remember and very beneficial to everyone. Again, you can use
them on yourself, your children, your partner, friends, pets or
anyone in need of balancing. These techniques are not meant to
replace the need of seeing a physician. They are to help you on a
daily basis or when needed to maintain balance and calm.

Tech. #1

Temples: Gently place the pointer and middle fingers of
your left hand on your left temple and the pointer and middle
fingers of your right hand on your right temple.

Center of the Forehead: Imagine a vertical line dividing
your face into left and right halves. Place the fingertips of each
hand on the corresponding side of that centerline, one half inch
below your hairline. Your fingertips of your right hand will be
on the right side of your forehead and your left fingertips on the
left side of your forehead.

Top Front of Head: Imagine your hair parted down the middle. Place the fingertips of each hand gently on each side of the part starting about one half inch above the hairline.

Base of Skull: Place the index and middle fingers of each hand at the base of your skull; about one half inch to each side of the spine.

Sides of the Face: Stretch your arms out in front of you. Bend them at the elbows, cross them, and spread your fingers apart. Place your fingertips on either side of your face, with your index fingers touching the spot where the top of your ear joins your head. Spread the fingers out evenly with the little fingers resting on your jawbone.

Back Crown of Head: Place your finger tips on either side of an imaginary vertical line running down the center of the back of your head from the crown to the spine. Your little fingers will rest on the top of your head, and the others follow the curve of the back of your head.

Hold each position approximately two minutes. You may need to hold some of these points longer than others because the flow of energy has more blocks and will take longer to correct. The more you use the technique, the better you will get at feeling the energy and how long you need to hold the points.

You do not have to use the same order all the time. If you don't have the book with you, use whatever points you remember. They will help you anyway. For example, a friend of mine was about to faint so I touched as many of the meridian points as I could remember and was able to stop her from passing out. The more you use these techniques the more you will remember and be able to use in times of need. You might try using this technique before you go to bed to help you have a better night's sleep.

Balancing the Mind and Body

I used these techniques, especially #3, on a daily basis when I was ill. The physicians couldn't figure out what was wrong nor could anyone else. My symptoms were: I'd collapse and was unable to move, open my eyes or talk. I could hear what was going on around me but couldn't respond. My brain felt like it was split in two and that right and left hemispheres were not communicating like they should. It became difficult for me to walk very far and eventually I had to quit working.

Every day I would touch the meridians in a specific order. Eventually it helped me regain enough strength that I was able to walk further each week. It didn't stop me from collapsing but several years later I was able to move a little bit while being down. I don't think I would have recovered as well as I have from this illness if it hadn't been for my working with the meridians to balance my body. I now believe that this illness was caused from exposure to toxic mold that developed when my condo was flooded by the breaking of the water heater. I also believe the mold caused kidney failure and killed my little dog.

If you have an illness that affects the nervous system, try using this technique on a daily basis. I don't guarantee it will work for everyone but it might help and remember these techniques will not harm you. Should you find some relief you might want to search out someone who uses these techniques in more depth. Find someone who works with meridians as well as other forms of healing such as Healing Touch and Acupuncture.

Tech. #2

Align the Mind

To align the mind, hold each of the following points for a minimum of two minutes, longer if you need to.

1. With the tips of the fingers on your right hand placed close together position them vertically on the back of your neck along the spine. Your little finger will be at the base of your skull and the pointer finger at shoulder level. Place the fingers of your left hand vertically at the center of your forehead. They will extend from the edge of your hairline to the top of your eyebrows.

2. Place the palms of both hands on the back of your head with the bottom edge of your hands along the base of your skull between your ears. Point the tips of your fingers towards the top of your head and touch the ridge of your skull where the head begins to flatten.

(If you are doing this on someone else who is lying down, your hands will be turned in the opposite direction. The tips of your fingers will be at the base of the skull and the edge of your palm will be towards the top of their head.)

3. Imagine a line that goes between your eyes, up your forehead, and over the top of your head. Place the palms of your hands on the top of our head on each side of this imaginary line that divides your head. Your fingers will point towards the back and rest on your head.

Instead of the palms, you can place your fingertips on the top of your head on each side of the imaginary line.

(If you are working on someone else, your hands will be turned in the opposite direction. Your finger tips will be towards the forehead and the edge of the palms, next to each other, towards the back of the head.)

4.   Using the tips of the first three fingers of each hand, place them vertically on each side of your head. Your pointer finger will be at the top edge of your ear where the skin connects to your head and the other two fingers will rest vertically above that. Do not cross your arms to do this position.

(When doing this to someone else, your ring finger will be at the top of the ear instead of the pointer finger.)

5.   Using the imaginary line that goes down the center of your face, place your fingertips vertically on your forehead on either side of the line between your eyebrows and your hairline.

6.   From position five, keep one finger at the hairline and spread your fingers apart slightly moving the little finger (at an angle) towards the outer edge of your eyebrow.

7.   Open and close your mouth slowly. With your index finger find the point where your upper and lower jaws come together and move. Gently massage this spot.

You can use this technique on people with headaches and dizziness. I wouldn't be surprised if this would also help children with learning problems because it helps the flow of energy through the brain. You may have to use the techniques daily for a while to notice any changes.

Tech. #3

Align the Body

To align the body, hold each position below for a couple of minutes or until you feel it's time to move to the next position. Your ability to know when to move on will increase as you get used to the sensations, or energy flow, in your body. During my healing process, this entire technique took me an hour to an hour and a half, but my body was very weak then. It will probably take you fifteen minutes or more, depending on what your body needs.

Here are the steps: ***Begin with the left side of your body:***

1. Place your right hand on the bottom of your left foot while placing your left hand around your ankle.
2. When you feel you are ready, move your right hand to your ankle and your left hand to your knee.
3. Move up your leg, right hand to your knee and the left to the hip joint.
4. Repeat the same steps on your right side, with your hands reversed (the left hand on the foot and the right hand on your ankle).

You have just walked your hands up each leg, one hand following the other, and now you are at your hips on the right side. Next take the left hand from your knee and place it on your left hip so that both hands are on your hips. Hold for your usual amount of time with hands on hips.

You are now ready to move up the center of your body.

5. Just below your genitals, place your right hand between your legs (1st chakra), palm facing towards your body. Place your left hand on your 2nd chakra, approximately two inches above your pelvic bone (for women, this is at the level of your ovaries). Hold.
6. Move your right hand to your 2nd chakra and place your left hand on your 3rd chakra at your naval.

7.   Remember, your right hand always moves to the position that your left hand has just left.

8.   Next, move your left hand to your heart center between your breasts, and place your right hand over your naval. You have now moved your hands over the first four chakras of your body.

The next position is **not** considered a major chakra, but it is just as important.

9.   Move your left hand to a point halfway between your heart center and your throat. This is called your "high heart" (thymus). Move your right hand to the position your left hand just vacated over your heart center. Hold.

10. While you are connecting energy between your heart and high heart you are connecting two areas that you may not have been aware of before. In fact you may experience a release of some emotion while holding this position. The high heart is the center for your purpose here on earth. Energy added here may also help to stimulate your body's immune system response.

11. Now move from the center of your body to your arms. As you may realize, you cannot do your arms as you did your legs. This is one of those times you could use a third arm. Not to worry.

Begin by putting your palms together, holding your hands.

12. Move the palms of your hands to cover the opposite wrists. Place the left palm on the right wrist and the right palm on the left wrist.

13. Next, move to your elbows. Place your left hand on the inside of your right elbow and your right hand on the outside of your left elbow.

14. Last, hold your shoulders. Place your right thumb on your right shoulder and the left thumb on your left shoulder.

Now, to finish, move back to your high heart.

15.   Place your right hand on your high heart, half way between your heart center and throat; place your left hand over your throat (5th chakra).

16.   Move your left hand to your forehead (6th chakra) and your right hand to your throat (5th) chakra.

17.   Place your left hand flat on the top of your head (7th chakra) and your right hand on your forehead (6th) chakra.

18.   The last position is the 8th chakra, which is approximately six to eight inches above your head (you don't need to know its exact location). Extend your left hand approximately three inches from the top of your head and turn your palm upwards. Place your right hand on top of your head. Now hold.

(This technique is explained so that you can perform it on yourself. But, you can also use it on someone else. The steps are the same except that when you do the arms, hold one arm at a time using the same steps as you did for the legs—hand and wrist, wrist and elbow, elbow and shoulder. Repeat for the other arm then move on to shoulder and shoulder just as you did for hip and hip. Now return to step 15 and continue up the body to finish.)

You can do a shorter version for aligning your body if you do not have the time for the entire technique. Place one hand on each hip joint and hold; move to the shoulders, placing one hand on each shoulder and hold.

This technique will help you to relax as well as balance your nervous system. Others have used body connection every day and found relief from migraine headaches, asthma, and other chronic illness.

Soothing the Body

It's important to keep the body relaxed and clear of tension, especially in the spine. The spine is a major nerve center that relates to many of the body's emotional, psychological and physical stresses. Energy moves through the spine to every part of you including your brain and higher centers. By keeping the spine area relaxed, centering and balancing will be easier.

Tech. #4

You can do this technique alone or with a partner. It's easiest done when lying down, but you can sit if necessary.

If you're alone, "imagine" a finger gently touching the top of your spine (no one will be physically touching you, but imagine that they are), where it connects to the base of the skull. Imagine a second finger gently touching the other side of the spine about a half-inch below the first finger. Move the first finger down the spine opposite the second finger, and a half-inch below it. Touch the spine there, and continue moving alternate fingers down each side of the spine at half-inch intervals. One finger will move slowly down one side of your spine while the other moves down the opposite side. It's as though your fingers are gently walking down your spine. Maintain at least half an inch between the contact points. Finish with a finger gently touching the base of the spine. As you move down the spine, you may hold some spots longer than others. The 4th, 3rd, 2nd, and 1st chakras are generally held longer than others. Hold any spot for as long as you feel it is necessary.

As you touch each of these spots, your body will slowly begin to relax. You may find yourself falling asleep before you finish.

❧

If you have a partner, follow the pattern described above using your pointer fingers to gently touch each side of the spine, moving slowly down at regular intervals of one-half to one inch. Then, if you haven't put them to sleep, have them do the same technique on your spine. Your children would probably love doing this simple technique on your back as they love touching. Try this on your children and see how it relaxes them.

Enjoy the feeling!

Chapter 2

STAYING CENTERED AND GROUNDED

Being In Your Body

Centering, sometimes called grounding, is enjoyable and useful process that can help you feel safe, calm, and more energetic. Being centered might feel uncomfortable at first if you're not accustomed to being in your body (that is having all your energy drawn and focused within). I have walked individuals, who have never centered themselves, through the Feet in the Sand technique #6. When we were finished I asked them to try moving their feet. They had a hard time; their feet felt like they were in cement. I asked them how their body felt. There were several responses, some said strange, heavy, and others said uncomfortable but solid. Their energy was drawn in, not scattered.

The reason you center or ground yourself is to keep your energy focused within your body. You will be less likely to trip or hurt yourself when you are centered. Being centered helps you be more aware of your surroundings. As you observe the world from inside your body you have a keen awareness that didn't exist before. Your intuitive, insightful messages also will become clearer.

It's always better to teach others how to center themselves instead of you centering them. It is not appropriate for you to center or ground others without asking permission first. You don't need to ask them person to person, you can ask their spirit. In your thoughts, and always with good intentions, say, "their name would it be alright if I ground you to help you stay safe?" If you get a yes then go ahead and ground them. But, if you get a no or even feel a hesitation then you must not ground them. When you are not given permission to ground them you'll find that no matter how hard you try the grounding technique it will not hold. Their safety is up to them not you. When you ground them against their wishes you are interfering with their choices about their life.

Learning What Is Effective

There are several centering or grounding techniques. Some are quick and easy while others will take a little longer until you become proficient with them. As you work with them you'll find the ones you like the best. Use whatever feels the most comfortable and works the best under the different circumstances. Some techniques are quicker than others so you may opt for them when there are time restrictions. Follow your inner feelings on which technique to use and when. You won't be wrong.

Tech. #5

Visualize a cord

Lie down or sit in a chair with your feet flat on the ground. Visualize a cord attached to your 1st chakra, your tailbone. The cord can take the form of a redwood tree, tall and straight; a beam of light in any color that you like; a heavy-duty chain; a rope, or any other solid image that occurs to you.

Feel the cord passing through the chair, the floor and going down into the earth. Attach the far end of the cord to an imaginary ring at the center of the earth, and feel or have it tighten. If you feel yourself being drawn down the cord, make the cord smaller in diameter. If you're having trouble getting the cord to go down to the center of the earth, make it larger in diameter, more solid, or pretend that someone (I often use fairies) is pulling the cord down for you. You may have to make adjustments when you first begin, but it will get easier and faster.

Once you are centered, your feet will feel firmly planted on the floor. Your body may feel strange, but it will feel solid. After you get used to centering yourself while seated or lying down, you'll be able to center yourself anywhere and any time.

Tech. #6

Feet in the Sand

This is the easiest and quickest centering technique.

Visualize yourself sitting or standing alone on a beautiful sandy beach. Imagine digging two holes in the sand and burying one foot in each hole. Draw the sand up around your ankles. (Once you're familiar with this visualization, you can take a shortcut and simply imagine your feet covered in sand.)

Imagine your feet chakra opening and "roots" growing from the center of your feet moving into the earth. From the large main root smaller shoots develop and spread into the ground in all directions. Think of tree or plant roots and visualize the same root system. Send the roots as deep as you desire.

How do your feet feel? If you sent the roots deep enough your feet should be firmly planted on the ground and difficult to move. Your body should feel solid and it might be difficult to stand or move. If you can't stand or move make the roots smaller and pull them upward so they aren't so deeply planted into the earth. You want to feel solid but not to the point of being unable to move.

Tech. #7

Take a Deep Breath

While seated, take a deep breath. Inhale first filling your abdomen and then your chest. Hold your breath to the count of four. Release the air through your nose, first from your abdomen, and finally from your chest. Repeat as many times as needed to help you feel relaxed, but no fewer than three times. Sit for as long as you can to help your body relax.

This is a great technique to use when you need to face someone that's difficult or you're not looking forward to facing. For example, you have a meeting with your boss, your teenager or just a meeting that you feel stressed about. Take a moment and take deep breaths just before you enter the room. It's never too late. Those deep breaths will help you any time and anywhere.

While you're inhaling and exhaling you can also add affirmations. With the intake of breath you can say, "In comes love" or "I breath in the Light". You may have heard of other verbiage; use any that is positive. On the exhale you can say, "I release the old" or "Out with the negative". Again use any affirmations you have heard of or that comes to mind.

Tech. #8

Carry Smoky Quartz

Carry a smoky quartz crystal with you. Bill, a dear friend of mine, kept running into objects, slamming his fingers, causing numerous wounds. Sound familiar? I gave him a smoky quartz crystal, not sure he'd even carry it with him, but I thought I'd give it a try. One day he came to me and said he'd slammed his finger in a file cabinet drawer, and he'd been angry with me. He thought the crystal hadn't worked. He said that since he'd started carrying the crystal he hadn't been hurt until that day. When he reached into his pocket to throw the crystal away, he discovered that it wasn't there! When he got home he found it on his dresser where he'd mindlessly left it. To my surprise, he went out and bought another bigger smoky quartz crystal.

Smokey quartz is used for grounding. It's a quartz crystal that looks as though someone blew smoke inside, thus "Smokey Quartz". Don't confuse it with a clear quartz crystal, which can make you feel spacey if you carry it in your pocket or wear it as a necklace. Smokey quartz can be carried on your person. If you have a child that gets hurt or seems a bit spacey at times get them a Smokey quartz crystal. You might find a Smokey quartz necklace or a little pouch for them to wear or carry with them. If you're not sure you want to get it for your child, try it for yourself first then if you're comfortable give it to your child. Again, test it with them. Put the crystal in their pocket and see how they act or whether or not they get hurt or fall. Then remove the crystal and watch for the results.

Don't forget that Smokey quartz is a crystal and needs to be cleared of energy too. (See Chapter 4, Other Clearing Techniques.)

Centering Objects

In addition to centering yourself, you can center others as well as objects. Here are some examples of things you can center: your children, mate, friends, pets, home, car, desk, telephone, computer, office, and bridges. Explore the possibilities by imagining how those beings or objects would benefit from centering.

Years ago in the San Francisco Bay area there was a fire in a very busy tunnel. A gas tanker exploded and sent a fireball through the entire tunnel killing several people. Someone later told me she was really uncomfortable driving through the tunnel and it seemed as though others were too. Since I lived on the other side of the Bay I personally wasn't affected by the tunnel. One day I had to visit someone requiring me to drive through the tunnel. I decided not to center or clear the energy before I got there as I wanted to know how the energy in the tunnel felt. I am very sensitive to energy and as I drew near the tunnel I could feel the fear and terror of those that had to drive through it on a daily basis. This tunnel is quite long and it was not a pleasant drive.

Before I returned home, and because I had to drive through the tunnel again, I sat down and centered the area. First I imagined several cords running from the bottom of the tunnel into the earth. Using several clearing techniques, such as vacuuming and sending in light from above and pushing the old energy down the centering cords, I cleared as much of the old energy out as I could. On my return through the tunnel it felt more comfortable. On several occasions I centered and cleared more of the energy to help those that had to travel through the tunnel feel safe again.

꙳

Another example:

My girlfriend wanted to keep her husband safe when he went on the ladder to paint the house. She remembered the grounding techniques I had taught her and decided to use them. She grounded the ladder and her husband using technique #5. He didn't fall or get hurt. By grounding the ladder my friend made it more secure and safer for her husband.

Other objects you can center and clear are your computer, bed, furniture or anything you think needs clearing. Attach a cord to the object, drawing the other end down to the center of the earth. Imagine gold energy filling the object, pushing the old energy down the cord into the earth or out into the universe and ask that the energy be transmuted to a higher vibration

Here's an example of how to ground your car.

Tech. #9

Traveling with Safety

Your personal safety and the safety of any vehicle in which you are riding can be enhanced by a centering technique. If you find yourself feeling uneasy, use this technique to center the car and clear its energy.

Visualize a cord firmly attached to the underside of the car at its center. Drop the cord down through the earth, and attach it to a ring located at the center of the earth. Imagine shorter cords connecting each tire to the main cord. Center the car, and run gold energy through every part of the car. Empty the old energy down the cord into the earth. You can also do this while driving.

After you center an object clear the energy by running gold energy through it.

These centering techniques are great tools to teach your children. You can teach a baby to center itself. (Babies and children are a lot more receptive than we give them credit for.) Talk the baby or child through the steps several times on separate occasions until you feel he or she has learned it. Thereafter, you can simply request that they center themselves, and their mind and body will remember how.

I suggest that you teach your family and friends these centering techniques. It is important to remember that it's not appropriate to center and ground those you love or whom ever you want to protect. You can do it occasionally when you feel eminent danger. But I add caution here because they have their own rules by which they live. You won't always be able to keep them safe. Neither is it your responsibility to make them safe. Let them be responsible for their own well-being as it is each person's responsibility to take good care of him or herself.

Chapter 3

HOW TO USE ENERGY

Running Energy

Once you have accomplished the centering process, you can replace old stuck energy from your body with new, clear, healing energy. You don't always need to center your body before you run energy. It's good to center and then run energy when you first learn these techniques. By combining both when you first learn you will help your body feel more comfortable and used to the energy changes or shifts. As you become more familiar with each process you'll find that you can center or run energy at any time.

You can run energy wherever you might be. Running energy through your body helps clear out the negative, unhealthy energy you have accumulated from others as well as your environment. It will also help you release stress and other toxic energies. This will help you in the healing process but will not heal you of physical ailments. Again, do not replace these techniques with consulting your health care provider. These techniques, and especially running healing energy through your body, will not cure you. Running healthy energy and clearing out negative energy will help you live a healthier and more calming life.

Adding Color

Your body and those of your family, friends and others, are more attune to certain colors of energy. At the same time individual bodies can have a negative response to other colors. The one color of energy that vibrates with all bodies is **gold**. You can run gold through your body and anyone else at anytime when you want to clear your body or theirs. **Rose**, associated with love, is another safe color. Rose color can be blended with gold. It is a soft and warm color that can be used at any time. Experiment with other colors on yourself such as yellow, green or even brown. Feel how each color makes your body feel. If you feel uncomfortable with one color then run gold through your body to clear that color out. Always run gold or gold and rose when you have finished experimenting. (It might be interesting to see how others react to you while running certain colors through your body.)

Don't use any color other than gold on someone else because you don't know how it will affect them. You wouldn't want to have them feeling uncomfortable and not knowing why. You could ruin their day by making them out of balance with a color that isn't attuned to their body.

Love, light and healing energy is one of the best energies to clear your body. Use what is comfortable and safe.

Tech. #10

Earth Energy Meets Gold Energy

With this technique you'll need to center yourself first. Center your body using a cord, Tech. #5. Open your feet chakras. Imagine or feel earth energy flowing into the center of your feet. (Have the earth energy come from deep within the earth. You don't want to use the surface energy due to all the pollutants and toxins in the soil.) Bring that energy up through your feet chakras, up your legs, all the way to your 1st chakra at the tailbone. Then have the earth energy return to the earth through the cord attached to your 1st chakra. A good way to visualize this energy flow is to pretend that the energy is flowing though imaginary pipes.

Now imagine bringing gold healing energy into your body through the crown (7th) chakra. Feel the gold energy flow into every cell of your body, pushing the old, negative energy into the earth. The gold energy will flow through your body and down the cord connected to your 1st chakra. Release the energy that is being pushed down your arms out through the hand chakras. Let the new energy flow through your body as long as you desire. Notice how different your body feels.

You can also blend different colors with the gold energy. Rose-colored energy, associated with love and the heart chakra, will add a very warm loving feeling. Experiment with different hues of blue or green for example. Some colors will have a calming affect while others may make you feel wired and jittery. Always use the colors that make you feel most comfortable.

Tech. #11

White Light at Your Navel

Center yourself with the cord, tech. #5, attached to the first chakra. Imagine white light entering your 3rd chakra at your navel. Cleanse the 3rd chakra; then bring the white light up to your 4th, 5th, and 6th chakras; and send it out through the crown (7th) chakra. Let the energy flow through your upper body for a couple of minutes.

While allowing the energy to continue flowing out of the crown chakra, return your attention to the 3rd chakra. Imagine the energy splitting into two paths as it enters your body. The first half continues through the upper chakras and out through the crown chakra. The second half of the energy will flow downward through your 2nd and 1st chakras. Once it reaches the first chakra it passes into the earth through the cord.

Stay with the flow of energy as long as you can. Again, you may feel slightly uncomfortable at first when you have this pure light flowing through your body. The more often you use this technique the more comfortable you will feel allowing you to use it for longer periods of time.

(White light is often associated with God, The Divine or Higher Power energy. Because of its intense power you might need to acclimatize your body to the vibration of white light. The more you use it the more comfortable you will be.)

Tech. #12

Love, Light and Healing Energy

This is my favorite:

Ask that love, light and healing energy flow through your body. Have the energy enter your body through the crown (7th) chakra. As the energy flows into your body imagine it flowing through your brain, eyes, nose, mouth, and tongue having it continue through your throat and neck. Imagine and verbalize the words in your mind, that the love, light and healing energy fill every muscle and every cell in your body. Continue to imagine the energy flowing down through your shoulders, arms and hands and flowing out through the tips of your fingers. Bring your thoughts back to your throat and imagine most of the energy flowing down through the rest of your body. Ask that the love, light and healing energy flow through your lungs, heart, stomach, gall bladder, kidneys, liver, intestines, sexual organs and all the muscles in your torso. Ask that every organ, muscle and cell be filled with this loving energy. Feel the energy continuing down through your thighs, calves and filling your feet. Have the energy flow out through your feet chakras into the earth. Ask mother earth to transmute the energy to a higher energy form. Thank the earth for helping you.

Notice how different your body feels. Do you have a sense of peace and love?

Having this loving energy flow through your body is a great way to start your day. When you wake up give thanks for all you have. Then use this technique and have love, light and healing energy flow through your body. If you desire, replace the healing energy with God or The Divine energy (white light). Either energy will help you start your day feeling peaceful.

This is also a great way to end your day. You may find that you will fall asleep before you've completed, don't worry, as you will find that the energy will keep flowing through your body even though you are asleep.

Enjoy the feeling!

Note:

This is very important to remember when running energy. Should the inside of your body begin to shake uncontrollably, like a shiver you can't stop, you have **excess energy** in your body. You may have opened your chakras too much and/or forgot to close them when you finished. When this happens, use **Dump that Energy** technique #19. The more you work with energy the more you need to be aware of how much enters your body. The more you work with the energy the better you'll know what works for you. There will be times you want extra energy flowing through your body but not all day long. Adjust the flow for your comfort and release any extra you have accumulated. Remember to close the chakras to approximately the size of a penny.

Reclaiming Your Energy

You and those around you carry the energy of others without knowing it. You pick up your partner's, children's and co-worker's energy every day. Energies at home are co-mingled and often it's hard to tell where your energy ends and your partner's or children's begin. Plus every one in your home picks up energy from those they have been around during the day. You and your family collect other's energy when you enter elevators, stores, schools, work, or restaurants. You then become the unintentional recipient of that other energy in the form of a headache, heartburn, or some other malady or illness. You won't be aware that you've taken on someone's energy but you do and will. Now add the energy of those you and your family collected during the day. Does your body feel uncomfortable and tired? Doesn't your home suddenly feel crowded; well, it is.

At the same time you are collecting other's energy you are giving your energy away. You won't be aware of whom you give your energy to or whom you are getting energy from. There is a constant co-mingling and exchange of energy between you and those around you. Now doesn't it make sense that you'd feel drained at the end of the day? Doesn't it make sense that your children are tired? Think of all the energy they encounter at school each day. Can you better understand why your partner is exhausted when they come home? Isn't it amazing that you can function at all?

Everyone exchanges energy on some level without his or her knowledge. The problem is that everyone's energy frequencies run at a different vibrational level. You can compare energy frequencies to automobiles. Individual energies run like a Volkswagen, a truck, a Chevrolet Corvette or a Masseratti. The mixing of the different vibrations will leave the body tired and drained. You can't expect to put a Volkswagen engine in a

Corvette and have it run properly. The same goes for you. You need to maintain your vibration level, which is different from every one else, in order to function properly.

When your energy is "zapped" (taking on or giving away energy) from an outside source, you feel drained. It's not necessary to know whose energy you are taking on or to whom you've given your energy, you can reclaim your energy as well as release the energy of others. Some of these techniques are so simple and quick you can use them any time and anywhere.

These are important techniques to teach to your family members as well.

Tech. #13

"Sun of Gold" Energy Boost

Want a pick-me-up during the day when you feel tired or stressed? You can use this technique wherever you are, you don't need to be sitting or lying down. It's so simple you can use it while walking down the street or even driving.

Visualize or just ask that a "sun of gold" be placed above your head. Repeat the following, "I ask that all my energy comes back to me from wherever I may have left it." The energy will begin returning to you from your mate, children, car, office, etc. (This is a great technique to use when traveling to help recover from jet lag.) You can also place a sun of gold over the heads of your children and even your pets and ask that all their energy return to them. If you were with someone and you still feel their presence, imagine a gold sun over their head and say, "I ask that all of their name energy goes back to them." The energy will leave you and return to them. (If you still can't get them out of your mind use one of the "Setting Energy Parameters" techniques.)

❧

The following story is a perfect example of how to benefit from the Sun of Gold:

Don used to come home from work tired, frustrated, and unable to forget about the paperwork piled on his desk. His friend Tina told him that she had a simple technique that she used daily to relax. Don said, "That's okay, I'll just take a nap." Tina said, "Come on, Don, just try this first, before you take your nap."

Tina told Don to sit back and relax. "Now bring a picture of the office into your mind," she instructed.

Imagine a gold sun over the office. Repeat the following phrase: "All the energy in and near my body that belongs to the office goes back to the office." Also, picture the pile of paper work you haven't completed, or the computer terminal. Repeat the phrase once more. Now ask that the energy that's in your body, which belongs to your co-workers, go back to them. Use the phrase, "I ask that all the energy in my body and aura go back to...." Finally, place a gold sun over your own head. Now say the following, "I ask that all my energy come back to me from wherever I may have left it."

Don couldn't believe it. He immediately began to feel better and he didn't need the nap to re-vitalize himself.

So, if you find yourself constantly thinking about your office, your work, computer, boss, or co-worker, place a gold sun over the object or the person's head. Send the energy back to where it belongs and more importantly reclaim your energy. You can use this technique after watching television. If the program you've just watched remains on your mind when you retire for the night, ask that all the energy belonging to that show go out of your body and return to the television. Visualize the energy returning to the television and back down the cable.

Do you hang onto the energy of a particular person (your parents, for example) in the belief that somehow it is beneficial or necessary? You are benefiting no one. You are only hurting yourself and them. They need to function from their energy just as you do from yours. Remember, it's difficult enough coping with your own "stuff" without the added confusion of someone else's issues or feelings. It's difficult for them to cope with their issues when they have your energy/issues mixed with theirs. They don't need your energy they need their own. And it's not up to you to fix or heal them or the situation. When your energy is clear you are in a better frame of mind to help others. You will make better decisions and see more clearly when you have all of your energy to work from.

Separate your energy from others as often as you can, it will help you feel better and physically stronger.

Always call your energy back from wherever you may have

left it and always send anyone's energy you may have collected back to them. If you are sensitive to energy, you may actually feel a rush flowing into you when using restoration techniques such as the gold sun. Even if you don't experience it in quite that way, you'll realize a change because you'll begin to feel less tired and more energized.

Tech. #14

Name Physical Traits

This is a really good technique to use when the "Gold Sun" technique isn't enough. Some individual's energy is more difficult to send back because they want to remain attached to you for whatever the reason. To further separate your energies you will use "positive" physical traits or characteristics. This helps to further distinguish you from him or her. Also, because the person may be more difficult to eliminate from your energy, be clear of your intent. It is your intent to bring your energy back to your body from their body and send their energy back to them from your body. Whenever you have clear intent, be sure you are coming from your heart. If you get mad because the person is hanging on and send your intent with that anger you won't be successful. Generally people hang on to someone because they want attention, to be noticed or possibly forgiven. When you send them your anger they will hang on until you accept or love them. I don't mean deep emotional love. I mean loving acceptance of who they are and that they exist.

Here's how it works. With loving intent use five to ten "**positive**" physical characteristic differences between you and someone else. You may need to name more than ten depending on how attached the individual is to your energy. The example below will help you. Avoid using negative terms to describe characteristics. For example, instead of saying, "I have long nails, and she doesn't have long nails," say, "I have long nails and her nails are short." Always use the verbiage, "My name is and her/his name is." This defines whom you are describing and whose energy belongs where.

> My name is Tony.
> I have blonde hair.
> Her name is Anne.
> She has brown hair.

My name is Tony.
I am a male.
Her name is Anne.
She is a female.

My name is Tony.
I have blue eyes.
Her name is Anne.
She has green eyes.

Other traits or characteristic differences that you can use are your age; whether you are married, single or divorced; number of siblings or children; where you live, by either the street, city or state; height or weight; or the type or number of pets. As you can see it's not just the physical characteristics of the body that distinguish you from others. You can include anything that is around you that is different from their surrounding. The more differences you come up with the better the separation of energies.

You may feel your energies separate or you may not. It's not necessary for you to feel the energy shifts within your body. (The more you work with energy the more sensitive you will become to feeling the energy changes.) Even though you don't feel a shift or change in your body, you should begin to feel better emotionally and physically. Eventually you will stop thinking about or feeling the presence of the other person.

Tech. #15

Send That Energy Packing

Here's how to release the identified and unidentified energy of others that you are carrying with you.

Visualize a box, trunk or balloon next to you. Then say out loud or in your mind, "I ask that all the energy in my body and aura that does not belong to me, go into the box, trunk or balloon." Fill the container, and once you feel that it is full, place it on the horizon and blow it up. You may also place it in an imaginary fire to release the energy. Ask that the energy be transmuted to a higher purpose. If you feel there is more energy to be released, you can either make the box larger, or bring in another container. Repeat the process until you feel all the excess energy has been released. Don't forget to blow up or burn the container, or the energy will remain in your surroundings, which defeats the purpose. You want to make sure that you remove all the negative energy from your environment.

This technique is very good when you need to release the energy of someone specific. Someone, for example, who is always on your mind or with whom you're having trouble coping. Place the box twenty feet away. Repeat, "All the energy in my body and aura belonging to_____, go into the box." Place the box on the horizon and blow it up. Imagine stars soaring up towards the sky as the energy disperses. You can also burn the energy in an imaginary fire. This process can be repeated as often as necessary until you feel cleared.

Setting Energy Parameters

Whose Issue Is It?

There will be times when you have a confrontation with someone and you walk away feeling confused. It's like you're not sure what that whole disagreement was about. You find that you don't understand why it happened nor do you know what to do about it. There is probably a good reason why you don't understand what happened nor do you know what to do.

Here's a simple technique to help you figure out whether or not you need to do something about the confrontation that occurred.

When something upsetting happens involving another individual, bring your energy into your heart center. Ask your Inner Self, "Is this my issue, or theirs?" Go with the first response, don't edit or second-guess yourself. If the answer is "theirs," release the unwanted energy from your body using any of the techniques for releasing energy. Depending on the intensity of the confrontation you may need to combine several techniques and repeat the process. What happened is the other individual threw their anger or distressed energy at you. You received it and are now carrying it in your body. Remember you exchange energy with others all the times. But when someone yells at you or even throws a hand jester, they are throwing their anger at you. You are now carrying that negative energy in your body. By releasing the negative energy you'll feel better.

If you find that you've released their negative energy and you're still upset, then you need to understand what issue the confrontation triggered for you. This is important when your boss calls you into their office. They will throw their angry energy at you and that's what needs to be released. If you're still upset once you released their energy from your body you need to examine why you're still upset. Did they make you feel incompetent? If so you'll need to heal those feelings. Get clear on what needs to be cleared from your body that belongs to someone else and what you need to heal that belongs to you.

When you've just had a confrontation and you are feeling uncomfortable, your Inner Self is trying to tell you it's not your issue. You are being guided to release the energy that belongs to someone else. This way you will be able to think more clearly and feel centered. This is important if you need to go back to your boss again. Instead of feeling angry and confused you will come from a place of strength because you'll be centered. Inner strength is inner power.

Examples of Receiving Other's Energy

Sally had a clash with her landlord regarding money. She felt frustrated and didn't believe the money issue had originated within her. That specific issue was characteristic of her husband, from whom she'd just separated. Since they'd lived together for five years, the money issue had begun to feel to Sally as though it were her own. She had reacted from her husband's point of view. So, she visualized a box and asked that any energy in her body that belonged to her husband go into the box. She then placed the full box on the horizon and blew it up. Sally repeated the process several times and quickly began to calm down.

Here's a story from my own life. My friend Holly came to visit me one day. I'd been lying down, not feeling quite myself. Holly visited for only a few minutes before we got into an argument. She left feeling very upset. A couple of hours later we talked on the phone. She told me that when she got in her car she'd asked herself if the issue was hers. She got a "no" answer. I, too, had asked myself if the issue was mine when Holly left, and I, too, had received a "no" response. Whose issue was it then? After talking about the incident, I realized that I'd picked up someone else's energy at a breakfast meeting I had attended that morning. That was the source of the negative energy I'd been feeling. I placed that individual's energy in a box and blew it up and immediately began to feel better. I called Holly back and told her what had happened and that it wasn't her issue.

I was traveling down a one-way street to my bank. A truck had backed into a parking space and pulled out going down the wrong way on the one-way street. The street was just wide enough for one lane and one row of parking. I pulled over as far as I could but due to the size of the truck it was nip and tuck. The passenger of the truck flipped a hand jester at me as they drove by. Obviously they didn't realize it was a one-way street. Needless to say I began feeling quite uncomfortable. As I continued doing errands I couldn't get rid of the uncomfortable feeling. I finally realized that the passenger threw a lot of anger at me along with her hand jester. It took me a couple of techniques to eliminate the energy from my body but I finally got myself centered again with my own energy.

When you receive energy from someone it can be very subtle, obvious or somewhere in between. Whatever the case it will affect you in a negative way. If you're feeling irritated, tired, or just ill at ease after talking with someone or having a confrontation ask yourself, "Is this my issue, or someone else's?" If it's theirs, release the energy from your body. If the issue is yours, then consider going deeper, working through the concern as a healing process. Always try to live within your own energy.

Tech. #16

Wall or Mirror Barrier

Often times when you go out you might feel one or a group of people sending negative energy towards you. You might be at a party, work or even a restaurant when this occurs. Instead of spending time trying to separate their energy from you use a wall as a barrier. Place an imaginary wall made of bricks, cement or anything you can imagine between you and them. The wall will block the energy coming at you. As they send the negative energy towards you it will be deflected off the wall and sent back to the person or persons sending it. Move the wall slowly away from you and back to them. This pushes the energy from your immediate surroundings so you and those around you won't feel uncomfortable. Your surroundings will remain peaceful and also allow others to approach you. At the same time you will make it so uncomfortable for the others that they may need to move. Be aware of how the energy affects others.

Instead of a brick wall you can use a mirror as the barrier. Imagine a mirror with the reflective side facing the other person or persons. Whatever energy they are throwing towards you will bounce off the mirror back to them. It will make them uncomfortable and they should turn or walk away from you. This is great to use if your partner has troubled energy while you are lying next to them trying to sleep. This is also a good technique to teach your child if they are being harassed at school. (Also, teach them protection techniques from Chapter 5.)

There are times when you have a conversation, discussion or argument in your mind that doesn't originate with you. It's as though you are caught in a revolving door about a topic that you're not interested in or something that doesn't really bother you. What do you do to stop it?

Tech. #17

Say "Good-bye"

Bob was standing at the kitchen window washing the dishes. Every once in a while he'd start to argue in his mind with Rachel. He'd try to tune out the argument, but it kept reappearing. It got so irritating that he nearly broke a couple of dishes. He interrupted the mental argument to question the reason for its existence. He couldn't find an explanation for being angry with Rachel, but the argument raged on. Then he decided to ask himself the all-important question: "Is this argument mine or hers?" The answer was "hers."

Bob realized that Rachel must be mad at him, but instead of calling him to discuss it in person, she was engaging him in a telepathic argument!

❧

Everyone can send messages telepathically. You don't need to pick up the phone to send your thoughts to someone. When the message is an angry one, however, the individual receiving it may not understand what is happening. They might think that the emotion originates within their mind but feel confused because they don't feel angry.

So what should you do when an argument is going on in your head? First of all, ask yourself "Is this my anger, or does it belong to the other person?" If you find that the anger is indeed coming from someone else, stop the argument. You can say, "Stop" or "wait a minute." Mentally command the other person to quit using your mind to stage a disagreement. Then begin to carry on a conversation with that person as though he or she were actually with you. Say "hello" to them. Thank them for coming by, but tell them that if they wish to talk to you or confront you with a problem, they should telephone or visit in person. Tell them it's not okay to carry on an argument in your head. Say "good-bye," and tell them they need to leave now.

Here's another way you can tell them to leave you alone. Send them a telepathic message by stating in your mind, "I'm sorry that you're upset. I don't know exactly why you're mad, but let's talk. You might not realize that I'm receiving these thoughts from you, but I am. So please take back your argument and angry energy. If you need to talk to me, please pick up the phone and call me or come and visit. I'd welcome the opportunity to clear up this matter, but not this way."

When you've completed your conversation take a moment to send their energy back to them. You can use "**Physical Traits**, tech. #14" or place their energy in a balloon. Send the balloon in the sky, blow it up or burn it in an imaginary fire. Transmute the energy to a higher vibration.

❧

These steps will generally end the confrontation in your mind. If it doesn't stop, call the other person. Ask them nicely if they're upset with you in any way. If they question your reason for asking, describe what you've just experienced. Explain that even though no conventional form of communication was used, the message came through loud and clear. Approach the situation with compassion. If you throw your own anger at the other person, it will only worsen the situation. Remember, the other person wants to be heard, not yelled at!

It's important to understand that everyone receives information telepathically, whether the message is an argument or words of love. Perhaps someday we'll all develop the ability to deliberately direct our communication in this way. Wouldn't that be nice? Then we'll just need to be certain that the communication we receive is intended for us and not someone else.

Tech. #18

You Talk Too Much

Remember the last time you were stuck on the phone with someone who just wouldn't stop talking? They talked forever about nothing, and the longer they kept you on the phone, the more anxious you got. The next time you find yourself in that situation, imagine brown energy flowing into your head through the 7th chakra, and continuing down through your body and out into the ground. Have a large amount of the brown energy flow through the ear that is in contact with the phone. The energy will fill your ear canal up to your eardrum. This will help block their energy from flowing into your ear. Eventually they will feel the block and end the call or give you an opening to end the call politely.

The more persistent your telephone partner is, the longer you'll need to run the brown energy through your body. The color brown helps you become more grounded in the body and will help you disconnect from other individuals. Remember to dump the excess brown energy after you hang up. If time permits, run gold or rose colored energy through your body to help you re-focus yourself and raise your vibration again.

Chapter 4

CLEARING ENERGY

Clearing Out Other's Energy

Energy is everywhere and in everything. Wherever you go your energy is mixing with other's energy. You will not only exchange energy with individuals you know but with complete strangers. This exchange of energy occurs while walking down the street, at work, entering an elevator, a restaurant, a classroom, at home, literally everywhere. Words don't need to be exchanged in order for the exchange of energy to occur.

For years you have been mixing and exchanging energy with others. This exchange can and will make you physically tired and irritable. An illness will often occur because your body is energetically out of balance. This is why it is important to clear the energy of other's from your body on a daily basis or as needed.

The following techniques will help you clear the energy of other's from your body, aura and your home. The most important aspect of these techniques is that you, your body and home will feel more comfortable and peaceful. You want your home to be comfortable because it's the only retreat you have on a day-to-day basis. These are simple techniques and can be used anywhere and anytime.

Tech. #19

Dump That Energy

This is an easy technique that can be used anywhere and you can be either sitting or standing. If you pick up a lot of negative energy at work you can use this technique at your desk or by making a quick trip to the restroom. Before you go to bed **"Dump that Energy"** will help you get rid of energy you have collected from your day as well as the energy collected while watching television or any other source. (Dumping energy is a great way to eliminate any excess energy that has entered your body. When you have excess energy flowing through your body, you will start to shake internally. It's like having uncontrollable shivers but you're not cold. This technique will help eliminate the excess energy.)

While standing bend over so the top of your head is facing the ground. Have your arms dangling with your fingertips towards the ground. Allow the excess energy to flow out of your body through your head and fingertips. Imagine a hole in the floor, like a well, going deep into the earth. Send the excess energy into the well and down into the earth. It's important that you imagine a well, or some other means of letting the energy out of your room. Let it be absorbed by the earth.

If you are sitting, bend over as far as you can and allow your arms to dangle at your side. Feel the energy flowing out of your body. (You can do this technique if you are in a wheel chair. Bend over as far as you can. Try to point your head as close to the ground as you can. The top of your head will probably be pointing somewhere across the room, but that's okay, the energy can still drain out of your body. Have the excess energy flow into an imaginary fire that's across the room. If possible, dangle your arms down the side of your chair so the energy can flow out your fingertips into the earth. If you're unable to dangle your hands have your palms face upwards and ask the energy to drain out into the universe.)

If you live in a high-rise or apartment building, visualize a pipe with a wide opening going from your floor down to the earth. You can either have the pipe go through the other dwellings below you or run along the outside of the building. If you have the pipe going though the other dwellings below, be sure to remove the pipe when you are finished clearing your energy. You don't want it and your energy cluttering up the space of those below you. Even if you dislike them it isn't appropriate to fill their space with your energy. You should always have spiritual courtesy towards others.

As you dump the energy you can have it flow into an imaginary fire or into a box. Remember to remove the box from your surroundings and transmute the energy.

Tech. #20

Push It Back, Right Back

Do you take on and act out the emotions of others? When individuals can't express their own emotions, or are in denial, they often transfer those emotions to someone who is close to them. If you're in a relationship, have a close friend, or work closely with people, you may be taking on the emotional blocks of others. When you feel uncomfortable about the emotions you're experiencing, or when your reactions to others do not seem appropriate ask yourself, "Do the emotions I am experiencing belong to me?" Trust the first thought that comes to mind. If the answer is no then send the energy back to that person. The energy can still be returned to the sender even though you're not sure whom it's coming from.

❧

Imagine that the unwanted emotions coming towards you are like waves. Put those waves in reverse, just as if you were running a movie backwards in slow motion. Imagine the waves rolling slowly away from you, sending the emotions back towards whomever they belong.

❧

Another way to send the energy back is to imagine a mirror between you and the other person. Have the reflective side facing away from you and towards them. As they throw their emotions at you the mirror will reflect them right back to him or her. You don't need to know who is sending you their emotions. All you need to know is that the emotions you are feeling don't belong to you. The mirror will deflect the energy away from you and that's all you need to do to protect yourself. (Release any energy you may have already accumulated.)

❧

It is not up to you to heal someone else's emotion. If you desire to help the person, ask that God's love or universal love be sent along with the return of their emotions. If you know the individual, ask them if they need to talk about the problem they are having difficulty coping with. You can always listen with an open heart and compassion but don't try to fix them or their situation. Always stand in love when other's emotions are involved.

Tech. #21

Gentle Hands

Imagine your hands extended out in front of you, gently pushing back unwanted energy or emotions. Ask that the emotional energy coming at you go back to where it came. Always return the energy with love.

It's important that you move the energy or emotions back toward their source gently so as not to overwhelm the individual with their impact. Then place a big rose between the individual and yourself to maintain separation. If you're comfortable doing so, "in your mind" tell that person you're not willing to take on their emotions. Make it clear that it's up to them to deal with his or her "stuff." By doing this you are sending a telepathic message to the individual. On some level they will get it.

Clearing Your Body

Your energy centers (chakras) become clogged with the energy of other's. The chakra's get clogged like the drainpipe in your kitchen sink. Whenever you dispose of garbage, a little residue remains inside the pipe and this residue builds and builds. Eventually you need to clean the pipes out. As your energy mixes with others a bit of their energy remains behind in your body and chakras. Eventually, your energy centers will also get over loaded and need to be cleared.

There are situations in which you want a connection with someone through your chakras. For example, when a couple is in love they will connect with each other through their heart (4th) chakra. Often they will also connect through the first, second, third and fifth chakras. (See meanings to understand why they connect on these levels.)

Problems arise when individuals that you are not in a relationship with "plug" into your energy centers and chakra(s). It could feel like they are sitting inside your chakra center or like they are plugged in to you. It's as though there is a cord or rope connecting the two of you together. This connection can happen with anyone you meet. If you don't want them in your energy centers then their energy needs to be cleared from your centers.

These are important techniques to use if you have a massage, Reiki, Healing Touch or any form of bodywork. In some instances a body worker might inadvertently transfer their energy into your body. If the body worker talks about him or her while working on you his/her energy will intensify and come through their hands into you. You don't want to carry their emotions in your body, after all you went to them to feel better. Be sure to clear their energy out as soon as you can.

Tech. #22

Rose Scrub

There's an endless supply of imaginary roses in the universe. Imagine reaching out to the universe and grabbing a bunch of beautiful roses. There are a variety of colors to choose from. Different colors have different meanings such as red for love and yellow for friendship. Two other great colors to use are pink and white. You can choose the color or trust that the right color roses will be available depending on what you're clearing.

Clear your body in sections starting with your head. Grab a bunch of roses from the universe. Visualize the roses being placed inside your body, moving in a circular motion to clean and clear any unwanted energy. Use a fresh bunch of roses with each section. You might need more than one bunch in a section, depending on how murky your energy is. When you finish with each section of your body, place the used roses into a basket or directly into an imaginary fire. When your entire body has been cleared, place the basket in an imaginary fire and burn them. You don't need to do the whole body every time. Clean whatever part of your body you feel is clogged.

This is also a great technique to use when your eyes are bothering you. Use one imaginary rose at a time. See the rose partially open and then move the rose into your eye. Move the rose around and go all the way to the optic nerve. Feel the rose collecting the stress that your eyes are feeling. If the eye is extremely irritated or tired repeat the process as often as needed using a new rose. Take a new rose and repeat the technique for the other eye. Dispose of the roses by placing them into an imaginary fire.

Burning the roses allows the old, negative energy to be transmuted to a higher vibration. It's always important to release and transmute the negative energy.

Tech. #23

Chakra Cleaning

You can cleanse one, two or all your chakras at a time. If you are cleansing all the chakras, start at the crown chakra and move down. Use a single rose for each chakra. Imagine the rose partially open. Place the rose into the chakra. Move the rose through the chakra from the front to the back then pulling it back out the front. If the chakra doesn't feel clear after one rose, repeat the process as many times as needed. Move onto the next chakra with a new rose. Continue until you feel that the chakras are cleared of unwanted energy.

When you finish, place the roses in an imaginary fire, allow it to burn and ask that it be transmuted to a higher vibration.

Tech. #24

Fire Hose or Laser Beam

This is another technique for clearing the chakras.

While sitting or lying down imagine a fire hose or laser beam. Aim the hose/laser down through the top of your head, your 7th chakra (crown). Open the fire hose or laser beam and see white light flowing into your body and continuing down through the body and out the 1st chakra (tailbone). From the back of your body point the hose/laser at the sixth chakra. The white light will flow from the back of your body through the chakra forcing the negative energy out through the front, flushing it out into the universe. Repeat the process down the body until you finish at the second chakra. Let the light flow through each chakra until you feel that it is cleared.

Another great time to clear your chakras is in the shower. Imagine the water washing away all the negative energy that's in and on your body. As the water flows over your crown chakra feel it flowing through your body, pushing the unwanted energy down the drain. Stand under the water for as long as you can and enjoy the cleansing. Enjoy the negative ions! (While in the shower I often get great insights, so be open to information that may come your way.)

Don't forget to ask that the universe transmute the old energy to a higher and more beautiful energy. When you've completed each chakra tell them to close down to the size of a quarter. If you would like any of the chakras to be open further or shut down smaller just specify which one and tell it to open or close to a certain diameter. For example: If your fourth, heart, chakra is wide open you might find other's pouring their hearts out to you. Or your emotional issues might come up and you find yourself very angry and/or crying. It's important to keep the chakras partially open so you are comfortable. You can always experiment with having the chakras open to varying degrees to see how it feels and how others relate to you.

Tech. #25

Vacuum Your Body

This is a great technique to clear your body. Imagine a vacuum cleaner with a hose attachment. The hose can either be attached to your body or a couple of inches away. To clear your body, start at the 7th chakra (top of your head) moving the vacuum hose slowly around the inside of your head. While clearing the energy in your body you can clear specific organs. Say you have trouble with a kidney. Have the vacuum clear the energy from your kidney. (This won't cure your kidney but it *may* help the healing process. I know it won't hurt you.) Imagine the vacuum sucking out all the cobwebs and "stuck" energy. Then, proceed through your entire body, vacuuming up whatever energy does not belong to you. Once you've finished with your body, vacuum your aura, the area around your body.

Another image to use is having a wide nozzle on the vacuum. The nozzle is wider than your body. Begin five to six inches above your head and drag the nozzle slowly down your body. End the clearing several inches below the bottom of your feet. This will clear the energy in your body and aura. You may have to repeat several times to completely clear the unwanted energy.

I often use this technique as I'm falling asleep.

A third approach is to have the nozzle pointing at the center of your body, around your navel. Imagine the vacuum pulling all the negative energy out of your body and into the vacuum. You might want to do both the front and back of your body.

When you've finished cleaning your body, imagine placing the vacuum on the horizon and exploding it! Or you can set the vacuum in an imaginary fire to burn and transmute the energy. Remember to ask the universe to put this energy to a higher use.

৵৳

The vacuum is a great technique if you or anyone you know has had to stay in the hospital. It will help clear out the nurse's, doctor's, visitor's and other patient's energy. If someone you know was in the hospital but they don't live near you, you can still help them clear their energy. Visualize the person and then imagine the vacuum clearing their body as described.

When other's energies are cleared from you, or someone you know, the body will feel better and heal quicker.

৵৳

Note:

Any time you've been around a group of people, it's important to clear your body of their energy. There may be times when you've been with only one person whose energy you need to clear. Whether you've been to a party, had a hectic day at work, been around relatives or anyone you don't get along with or been anywhere you might have picked up negative or unhealthy energy. If you feel tired and haven't done anything strenuous then chances are that you are tired from the energy of others. Don't forget that giving away your energy will also make you tired. Use these techniques and run loving and healing energy through your body to help you recover.

Removing Energy from Your Environment

Everywhere one goes they leave a part of their energy behind. The more time spent in an area the more energy left behind. You'll find more energy of others on airplanes, workstations, restaurants, hospitals and retail stores. The environment is saturated with other's energy. When they come into your milieu they will not only deposit their energy but also the energy they have picked up along the way. This energy will affect you without your knowledge and it is important that you clear it.

Here's an example of how negative energy can affect you:
Michael entered the room silently. In the darkness, the room felt cluttered, as though there were others right there with him. He switched on the light, but no one was there. Yet the room still had an uncomfortable feel to it, similar to what he'd been sensing at his office lately. The office felt as though people were there even after everyone had gone home for the day. He thought, "Why is it that Judy's home always feels clear and clean? I wonder if there's anything I can do to make my own surroundings more comfortable and welcoming?"

Most people aren't consciously aware of why a room feels a certain way. They just know that they're either comfortable or uncomfortable. Whenever an individual leaves an area, part of them, in the form of energy, remains behind. Remnant energy accumulates and can make a place feel gloomy or crowded. For example, you might walk into a room in which an argument took place earlier or even the previous day. The room gives you an uneasy feeling and you don't know why. The discomfort you are feeling is the angry energy of the individuals involved. As they argued they sent angry energy flying around the room. They may have left the room but the negative energy remained. Now you are standing in that energy and feel uncomfortable. It's essential for you to clear your energy and if possible the room's energy.

Second hand clothing stores are filled with the energy of others. Every garment in the store has some energy of the individual that wore it. It's difficult for me to go into second hand clothing store for very long and impossible for me to wear any clothing someone else wore. I remember going into a store with my girlfriend, I had to walk back out again. Although there were only three people in the store (my friend, the employee, and myself) the store felt crowded. It felt as though there were hundreds of people in the store. Everyone left a part of themselves in the clothes they gave away and I felt them. If you wear second hand clothes and you feel emotionally or physically different when you put them on, you're picking up the previous owners energy. You might not be able to wear other's clothing, if you do, wash and or smudge the clothes with incense. Clear out as much of their energy as you can, so you feel comfortable wearing the garments.

Everyone's energy "fingerprints" are not only on clothes, they are left on everything wherever they go. When someone sits on your furniture they leave a part of themselves behind. As people come and go from your home or office they leave bits and pieces of their energy behind. To clear the energy from your home, office, or any room, use the following techniques. This will keep your milieu comfortable and clear of undesirable energy, including any negative energy you've collected.

There are many objects that can affect your environment in a negative way without your realizing it. Our bedroom in our new home felt uncomfortable and was difficult for me to stay in for long. I searched the room and the only object whose energy felt strange was the dream catcher that someone gave me which they had made. I removed the dream catcher and the energy shifted but it still wasn't completely comfortable in the room. Several months later I remembered that I had a similar situation years earlier. At that time I removed a nail from the wall that was left behind by the prior tenant. Once the nail was removed the energy shifted dramatically. I realized that the nail that held the dream catcher was still in the wall. As soon as I pulled the nail out the room immediately felt calmer.

If you have a room that feels uncomfortable, look at the objects in the room, including anything on the walls and ceiling. Remove items such as nails or plants left behind by the prior occupant. Also, clean the carpets as they will hold the energy of prior occupants too. The smallest item can hold negative energy. Look carefully and remove anything from the room that you feel might be holding negative energy. You might have to remove items and then check to see how the room feels. It might be a matter of hunting and removing different items to find the one causing the uncomfortable feeling that you are having. Once you find the right object you'll know because the room will feel better.

It's important to keep your environment clear. If you can, clear your home from negative energy on a weekly basis. It will feel more comfortable and peaceful and so will you.

Tech. #26

Vacuum Your Surroundings

Besides vacuuming your body you can vacuum your surroundings. Use an imaginary vacuum to clear the energy from a room, workspace, car or anywhere you want energy cleared. Imagine a vacuum outside the perimeter that you want to clear. Have the nozzle of the hose inside the space and vacuum the negative energy. Move it around the space and have it collect energy from objects within the space. Once completed, place the vacuum and the hose in an imaginary fire and transmute the energy. If you desire, fill the space with gold or gold and rose energy. The gold energy is compatible with your energy and the rose adds a touch of love.

(A few books on color are: *Mystery of Color* by Rosemary S. Friedman; *Healing with Color Zone Therapy* by Joseph Corvo and Lillian Verner-Bonds; *Color Magic for Beginners* by Richard Webster. For further information on colors, check out the Internet or book stores.)

Tech. #27

The Well

Imagine a well, or a deep hole, in the center of your room. (You can do this technique in all the rooms in your home or whatever room you feel needs clearing.) The opening of the well is about a foot in diameter. Imagine filling the room with gold energy coming from the universe. As the room fills with the gold energy it will push the old unwanted energy that's in the room down the well into the earth. Ask Mother Earth to transmute this energy to a more loving energy. You can also combine other colors with the gold such as rose and white. (Be careful not to use a lot of white light to clear a room. I used pure white light to clear my bedroom and couldn't enter the room for two days.) When you have completed clearing the room, close the opening of the well. Either ask the well to close or visualize it actually closing.

The room will feel calmer and more comfortable to be in.

Tech. #28

Two Sheets of Gold

Gold is the color that resonates with all human beings. It's always safe to use gold whenever or wherever you want to clear energy. With this technique you can clear a single room, the whole house or whatever space that needs clearing.

Imagine two sheets of gold spread out, one above the area to be cleared and the other below. Slowly move the bottom gold sheet upward through the area. Place the sheet of gold filled with the negative, unwanted energy into an imaginary fire. Then bring the top gold sheet slowly down through the area. Toss the second sheet into the fire to burn. Ask that the energy be transmuted to a higher form. Repeat the process until you feel the room cleared making it calmer and more peaceful.

Tech. #29

Burn Incense or Sage

Burning incense or sage (called smudging) will help clear any environment quickly and easily. If possible, burn incense (cone or stick) or sage on a weekly basis or as often as necessary in your home. Don't overlook the bathroom, closets, shower, or any other enclosed area where energy can be left behind. Remember you don't have to have anyone come into your home to accumulate others' energy. As you go through your day you accumulate others energy and then you go home and dump it. That's why it's important to clear the energy at home as often as possible.

There is a lot of sweet smelling incense available and these are great if you want to refresh the air. But if you want to clear negative, unwanted energy it's best to use incense that has more of a spiritual undertone. Native Americans use sage for smudging in their ceremonies. Other incense to use is Nag Champa (my favorite), Dalai Lama's Blessing, Pancha Buddha, Tibetan Monastery, Gonesh as well as sandalwood. These are just a few of the many kinds of incense available that can be used for the special purpose of clearing. If available, purchase blessed incense from a church or monastery. All of these will clear the energy and makes the area feel peaceful and loving. When cleansing a room you might need to use two or three sticks depending on size and what the room is used for. Burn one stick or cone to check how the space feels. If it's not completely clear then you'll need more. If you had a party you'll need several around the room and in the center to clear the entire space. (Incense releases a lot of smoke so be careful not to set off smoke or fire alarms.)

A lot of incense holders aren't required. If you have plants, place the stick or cone in or on the soil. Or use small cups or containers and place rice, sugar or salt in them to hold the incense. The cups will also catch the portion of the incense that burns and falls off.

(Here are a few web sites where you can buy incense: **Santosha.com; Spiritualscents.com; Incensewarehouse. com; MJGdesigns.com;** and **E-bay.com**.)

Other Clearing Techniques

The following techniques will also help you eliminate unwanted negative energy.

Tech. #30

Flowers

Place flowers in your home or office. Not only will they help clear the energy but will make your space beautiful. Roses and carnations are great for cleaning any negative energy that may have accumulated in your environment. The flowers will absorb the energy. If there is a significant amount of negative energy the flowers will probably wilt and die quickly. If that happens you might want to consider other forms of clearing such as incense so your flowers will last longer.

Tech. #31

Sea Salt

Your living space and objects accumulate energy from everyone that passes by or through. Sea salt is an inexpensive way to clear the unwanted energy. Sea salt will cleanse rooms, jewelry, crystals and precious stones. Here's just a few ways to use sea salt:

In the space you now live in or before you move into a new home or apartment, toss sea salt in the corners of each room. If the room is carpeted sprinkle the sea salt around the entire room. If you can, leave it for a week before you vacuum or sweep up. This will help eliminate the energy of those that have visited you and the energy of those who moved out of the home you're moving into.

❧

Combine the tossing of sea salt and the burning of incense for greater effect.

❧

Jewelry will accumulate energy while your wear it and from the people you are around or even pass by. It collects negative energy when you are upset and positive energy when you're happy. Even though you take the jewelry off the energy will remain. You don't want to wear jewelry that has negative energy because it can affect you. To rid jewelry from negative energy place them in sea salt. Bury the jewelry if you can and leave it for a couple of days. Sea salt should not damage your jewelry but if there's any doubt ask your jeweler.

❧

Crystals and precious stones will accumulate energy from you and others. The crystals and precious stones you have around the house as well as those in the jewelry you wear collect energy. They collect the energy of those who enter your home, the energy that you collected during the day. They collect the energy you throw out when you are angry or sad. Some crystals magnify the energy they collect. If you had a fight in your home the crystals will collect that energy and magnify it. That is why it's so important to clean your jewelry and crystals often. You don't want to live in or wear the negative emotions that the crystals collect. If you can, bury all or part of the crystals in sea salt to eliminate the negative energy.

Use the sea salt once or twice when clearing jewelry or crystals. As the sea salt accumulates negative energy it becomes saturated. The sea salt can absorb so much before it needs to be freshened.

Tech. #32

Cold Water

This is an important technique for anyone who does massage, Reiki or any other form of energy work. As you work on your clients your hands will accumulate their energy. Between each client and especially at the end of the day, run cold or slightly tepid water over your wrists. Let the water run over your wrists, down your palms and into the sink. Turn your hands over and rinse the back as well but the most important area is the wrist and palms. As the water runs over your wrists and palms it will wash away the energy you accumulated from each client.

Even if you don't work on others on a daily basis you can use this technique. You might shake someone's hand or maybe you gave a mini back or shoulders rub to a co-worker, friend or family member. They may have had a tough day or picked up someone's energy that needs clearing from their body. You don't want to hang on to that energy either. Rinse your wrists and hands with water and it will clear out the negative energy and feelings that you pick up.

Remember energy is in everything and as you touch each item you will collect some of that energy with your hands. Clearing is as simple as washing your hands but don't forget to include your wrists.

Tech. #33

Oil, Essences, Aromatherapy

There are some wonderful oils, essences, and aromatherapies to help you overcome unbalanced emotions. You can either create a desired emotion (calm, harmony, clarity of mind) or you can use these products to clear away negative emotions (sadness and hopelessness). Such products help you on many levels besides the emotional. You can find these oils, essences and aromatherapies at any health food store as well as most spas and the internet.

Some of these oils are quite potent and you need to be aware of how they make you feel. If, after using an oil and you find yourself feeling slightly spacey or light headed use "**Align the Mind**" technique #2 or any of the centering techniques to help ground you. You don't want to drive a car in this condition. You can get yourself centered wherever you might be. If you're driving, pull over or if it's safe, use one hand and "**Align the Mind**" the best you can. The easiest and fastest way to get grounded is by placing the tips of your fingers along the centerline on the top of your head. Place your thumb on one side of the centerline and your fingertips on the other side. This should be enough until you can pull over and use both hands.

Always be aware of how these different oils and essences affect you. If you start to feel uncomfortable in any way, rinse or wipe the oil off. You don't want to feel uncomfortable the rest of the day. Years ago I was at a breakfast with other body workers. Before I could stop her, a woman placed a drop of oil on my sixth chakra. I have no idea what the oil contained but when I got home I began feeling irritable and angry. The result was my girlfriend and I had an argument. Everything felt so surreal. When I thought back as to why I was feeling this way the oil that was placed on my sixth chakra came to mind. Picking up a towel I wiped the oil off and my mood immediately shifted. I've never heard of anything affecting someone like that but obviously there are some oils that don't mix well with everyone. As with medicine, oils can have some adverse affects on different individuals.

Here are some web sites for Aromatherapy and oils: **Newdirectionsaromatics.com;   Wellingtonfragrance.com; Dreamingearth.com;   Aromatherapyoutlet.com;   and Aromatherapywebsite.com**

Be cautious but also enjoy.

Tech. #34

High Vibrational Sound

A beautiful, musical method to clearing energy is to create healing sounds. Different sounds or musical notes vibrate at different levels. Your body and chakras also vibrate at different levels. Therefore, different sounds will affect you in a different way than someone else. You may find that you like a particular musician but for some reason your friend is uncomfortable when they listen to him or her. The reason is the vibrational level at which the artist is playing does not blend well with their body's vibration.

Here are some of the musical healing sounds you can use. There are Tibetan overtone chanting, Conch bells, crystal bowls, Gregorian chant, Native American drums and Chakra Chimes to help clear a room or your body. The seven Chakras vibrate at different levels and the Chakra Chimes are tuned to match each one.

Test the different sounds and notice how your body responds. Experiment with the various tools to find what fits best for you. Everyone connects with different modalities and approaches to healing according to what their inner guidance/ Spirit desires.

Have fun!

These items can be found on the Internet or your local metaphysical store. Here's a list of a few websites. Crystal Bowls: **crystalsingingbowls.com; bestbowls.com** and **discoverthesound.com**. There are cd's: *Sounds for Healing/ Crystal* and *Tibetan Singing Bowls* by Rainer Tillman and Crystal *Singing Bowl Meditation* by Margaret Ann Lembo. Chakra

Chimes: **soulvibs.com** and **spiritwinds.net**. Tibetan Bells: **beinginharmony.com.**

Chapter 5

PROTECTING YOURSELF

Now that you've learned how to center yourself and have cleared your energy, use any of the following protection techniques on a daily basis. They are handy whenever you're in an uncomfortable situation. You can use them for yourself, your children, your pet, your home, or any other person or object.

Adding Light and Color

Light and color help to heal and protect you. For example, I have to be very careful when walking into a hospital because I'm very sensitive to energies. One day I entered a hospital to help a friend of a friend. He wanted me to do some Healing Touch on him. As I entered the hospital I could feel the illness, pain and sadness of the patients. It felt as though some of the patients knew there was a healthy person walking down the hall and wanted some of that energy. After visiting my friend's friend I left as fast as I could. Now when I enter a hospital, thrift stores or anywhere there are a lot of people or where their energy was left behind I surround myself with protection.

You may have had similar feelings when you visited a hospital or some place that was crowded. Afterwards, you felt drained or uncomfortable from picking up others energy. Even if you aren't sensitive to the draining or taking on of energies it's important to protect yourself. Protecting you will help in maintaining your energy level. The need for releasing and reclaiming your energy will be reduced.

These protection techniques are very simple and can be put in place at a moments notice.

Tech. #35

Bubbled Dome

The bubbled dome is a great way to protect your home, apartment, condo, duplex and body.

ক্ষ

At your current home or whenever you move to a new home imagine a bubbled dome around the entire property. Have the dome end at the property line and extend as high into the sky as you want. If you live in an apartment, condo or duplex imagine it surrounded by a bubble. Have the bubble fill the walls, ceiling and floor between your apartment or space and those next to, above and below you. Your intention is to enclose your home and property inside the dome.

After you have the dome in position, add an imaginary rose in front of each door for further protection. Pretend the roses are your gatekeepers. When you first begin protecting your home you might want to check in and see if the roses need replacing or if the dome has come down. The more you work with the dome the stronger the connection you will have. It's like a baby learning to walk the more they practice the easier it is. Eventually they walk on their own and don't need help. When you aren't used to working with energy you need to practice. When you are clear about having a dome in place all you'll need to do is put it in place once and not worry about it again. The same goes for the roses. When I first started I checked the roses every few weeks or months, now I no longer need to check. In order for you to check the roses, imagine yourself looking at your door from the outside of the house. If you see or feel that the rose is holding excess energy, replace it. If it feels like the dome came down replace it. You can replace the dome and roses anytime you want or need to.

I have been using this technique for years. Whenever I move I put up a dome and I have never had a break in. I will not guarantee that you won't have a break in but try it and see how your home feels.

Your physical body needs protection as well. The same technique applies. Surround your body with a bubbled dome that extends about two feet away from the body. Have the dome extend two to three feet above your head and below your feet. The dome should include your aura. If you have the dome too close to your body you may feel uncomfortable, almost claustrophobic. If you have the slightest discomfort, extend the dome further away from your body. Or you can ask your aura to come in closer to your body (approx. twelve inches). You might want to play with the distance to find the most comfortable placement of the dome. For example have the dome five feet from your body and then slowly imagine it coming closer and closer. The moment you feel uncomfortable move the dome back out a little ways. Now bring it slowly back towards your body and the moment you feel uncomfortable move it back a little until you are comfortable again and leave it there. This should make you feel comfortable and safe.

For additional protection place a gold mesh, blue or white light and/or flowers on the outside of the dome. It's like decorating or painting your home. It adds, unseen to the naked eye but never the less, beauty for you. You can also experiment with the different colors around your body dome. Place blue light around the dome and then walk down the street or go to a party. Next try roses and see what affect that has on the people you meet. Do people actually respond differently? The response might be so subtle that it's unnoticeable. If you don't see any difference in how others respond to you then decorate the dome in a way that's fun for you.

Tech. #36

White or Golden Light

When you first use this technique you might want to sit or lie down. This will help you concentrate and feel the energy.

Using a ray of white or golden light coming from the universe or heaven is another approach to protecting your body. Allow the light to surround and quietly fill your entire body and aura. Remain silent for as long as you can while the light flows through your body and around you. You can also add a band of blue light to the perimeter of the white or gold light. This helps soften the intensity of the white light.

When you use this technique watch how others react or respond to you. See if strangers approach you or move to the side. Experiment with this technique and you'll know when it's appropriate to use and when not to.

Tech. #37

Silver Dome

The silver dome is probably the strongest form of protection you can use. Use this technique if you're in a very uncomfortable or unsafe situation.

Visualize a silver dome around your body and aura. Extend the dome several feet away from you, above and below you. Think of yourself encased in an invisible steel room that moves with you. The silver dome has a "closing down" or "cloaking" effect, rendering you almost invisible. For additional protection add spikes to the outside of the dome to ward off any potential hostile aggressors. **(I cannot guarantee this will work if you find yourself in an extremely dangerous situation. I have not been able to test it in those circumstances and I didn't know this technique when I was raped. All I can say is try it. The silver dome, with spikes, might be enough to get you to safety.)**

This is another technique that would warrant experimenting with. Put the silver dome around you, go out for a walk and watch how others respond. Then add the spikes to the dome and beware of the reactions you receive. You might not see a reaction or response, it might be subtle or you might see others moving out of your way. Remember some people are more aware of the energy around them while others are not. Also, most people are not consciously aware of the different energies around them yet they will still respond. The only way you'll know is through experimentation.

If you run or walk alone you might want to protect yourself using one of these techniques, especially the silver dome. On the other hand if you go out and want to meet someone these may not be the techniques to use. If you go out and want to meet others and still protect yourself, experiment with the white or golden light with the blue around the edge. The more you experiment with these techniques the better you'll know when and when not to use them. You want to protect yourself not drive people away.

Just because you use these techniques, don't assume that you can place yourself in dangerous or risky situations. Continue to use good, practical judgment in whatever you do. Always follow your intuitive or gut feelings. If you feel uncomfortable in someone's presence, leave as soon as you can.

"Your consciousness is your best protection," says Sai Baba.

The Power of Imaginary Roses

Prevent an Accident

The following techniques will give you several ways in which to help protect you from accidents. They will also help protect you from the aggressive energy of other drivers.

Tech. #38

Tailgaters

I taught this technique to several of my friends who were so amazed at how well it worked. Use this technique while you are driving or riding with someone else. This technique will stop tailgaters, whether the tailgater is coming at you from behind or if you're riding with someone who is tailgating. When someone is tailgating your car imagine two or three roses in a line between your car and the one behind. Line the rose up from left to right or spaced directly in the middle of the back of your car between your back bumper and their front bumper. The car tailgating yours will either back off or go around as soon as possible.

When you are riding with someone who is tailgating imagine two to three roses in a line, same as above, between your car and the one in front. The individual driving the car you're in will either back off or go around the car in front. It's so simple yet it works.

Tech. #39

Aggressive Drivers

If you feel aggressive energy coming from the driver behind you or if someone is approaching too fast, place imaginary roses between your cars. The roses will absorb the energy that's being thrown at you. The car will hopefully go around you when it's safe.

Surrounding your car with roses also helps when you feel that the car next to you might come into your lane. When I lived in the Bay Area I had to drive across the Golden Gate Bridge to get to work. The commute traffic on the Golden Gate Bridge can make you feel very nervous. When I commuted across the Bridge the only thing separating me from on coming traffic were orange cones. They had to move them from one lane to the next to allow four lanes going one way and two the other during commute hours. During normal hours there were three lanes in each direction but again only the orange cones separated the lanes, which caused many head-on accidents. When I felt uncomfortable and sensed that a driver was too close, a bit erratic or in too much of a hurry, I would surround my car with roses to feel safer. Thank goodness I never had an accident.

Note: If you feel aggressive energy from the driver behind you in addition to the roses, use a mirror. Place an imaginary mirror between your cars with the reflective side facing the driver behind you. The mirror will reflect the aggressive energy back to them. Don't forget to get rid of the aggressive energy that you received when they first approached you. If you retain that negative energy you may find yourself becoming an aggressive driver. The negative energy will continue to get passed on from driver to driver. That makes for very unsafe driving conditions.

Be safe and be healthy!

❧

Note:

These techniques help distance you from other aggressive drivers but are not a guarantee there won't be an accident. Sometimes the universe has other things in store for you and nothing will help. For example: Years ago I was invited to a party at Stinson Beach. I had a very uncomfortable feeling all the way there. To protect my car I use a cord to center it and placed roses all the way around it. When I got to the party everyone was parking partly in the ditch and partly on the road due to how narrow the road was. As I parked I had a really bad feeling but since someone was parking in front of me I kept the car where it was. Later that night I walked out on the porch and saw a motor home driving up the road and thought "I hope he can make it through all these cars." There were no streetlights so it was difficult to see anything when I got to my car. I started the car and looked in my side mirror before I pulled out. Well I couldn't see my side mirror. I rolled down the window and much to my surprise there was no side mirror. Obviously the motor home clipped my car breaking the mirror. All the protection of roses and the dome didn't help. I figured that there was some karmic pay back or something between the owner of the motor home and myself. It was the funniest experience. It felt as though I had gone out on the porch to say, "Hi," to the owner of the motor home, and told him that since my car was up the street on the right he should go ahead and pay me back. The point being is that protection doesn't always keep you safe, most of the time it will, but not always. There might be something that your spirit wants you to experience or an agreement that needs to be completed that you don't know about.

Don't be distraught if the technique doesn't work. Most of the time it will but as I said, you might have a lesson you need to learn or some type of universal pay back. As we live we learn.

When You Feel Overpowered

There are times when you might feel overpowered by someone. It can be your boss when they are telling you something you may have done incorrectly, a partner when you're having an argument or when you're out in public and someone is angry. You might feel as though you are being bombarded with baseballs or you might feel like there's a giant hovering over you. Either way you might feel like it's difficult to get away from the person that makes you uncomfortable. But there are ways to help protect yourself and possibly make them back off.

Tech. #40

When you are feeling overpowered imagine a circle of roses around you. Make sure the roses are between you and your aggressor. You can place them about waist high and, if the space allows, about a foot away from your body. (Depending on the circumstances you might want to have the roses go from the floor to the top of your head. This will give you more protection than just having them circle you at your waist.) If the person is right next to you place the roses between you and then move the roses out away from your body. The person should move away as the roses move away from you. This might be difficult at first because you are feeling overpowered so it's a good idea to practice this technique. This is especially good exercise to practice if you have someone in your life that is often aggressive towards you. That way when they come at you the technique will be easier for you to remember and use while you're in the middle of the discussion.

A woman I used to work with taught this technique to her daughter Valerie. Valerie was frequently victimized by her father's playful pinches. One night, as Valerie's father was about to pinch her, she imagined being surrounded by roses. To her surprise and satisfaction, her father stopped in mid-attack and left her alone. I believe her daughter was nine at the time. It's a great technique to teach your children as well. Children don't always tell when they have someone at school that's being aggressive towards them. By teaching them these techniques they can better protect themselves. It's always good to empower children no matter how simple the form.

You can also use the mirror with this technique. Have the mirror reflect the aggressor's energy back to them.

Don't Touch My Tummy

Because I've never been pregnant I can't be sure how well this technique will work. But I know that rose protection works. People have such an attraction, admiration or are just in awe of pregnancy that they always want to touch a pregnant stomach. I think we are all fascinated with the fact that a baby grows within the body that we want to be as close to or touch it whenever possible. We just seem to be fascinated with the miracle of a being developing within a body. But, I'm sure that women get tired of being touched when they are pregnant. So here's a little help.

Tech. #41

Before you go out in public imagine a big, open rose facing away from your body. (You can imagine the roses as you get out of your car or before you enter a building. You can do it at the last minute as well. Even if you're not sure they will touch you and you see someone coming towards you put the roses up.) Place the rose directly in front of your tummy. Make the rose as big as you want to help protect yourself. For further protection place a rose on each side of your stomach. You can also surround your body with roses, having them the full height and width of your tummy. Have the roses about twelve inches or more from your body. This should give you the privacy you deserve for your body as well as that of your baby.

Create a Clear Space

In the Park, or Anywhere

This is a great technique when you want some distance between you and others at a park, a movie or anywhere. Here's how you can protect your area without offending the people around you. I've never lived in New York so I'm not sure how well this will work with a population that large. But I do know this technique works.

Tech. #42

When you go to the park find the space you'd like for yourself. Sit in the middle of the space and imagine roses growing in a circle around you. Have the roses extend from the ground to approximately four feet high. If the roses are too close to the ground people might step over them instead of going around them. Place the perimeter of the roses five to ten feet away from where you are sitting. If the park is crowded you may have to bring the perimeter in a little closer. This should keep individuals from walking through your designated space and bothering you. If someone happens to walk through the perimeter watch to see if they look back with a strange expression on their face. They may have felt something strange as they walked through but not sure what it was. (Remember this is about energy. Everyone feels something but not always sure what he or she is feeling.) One day I went to a park and placed roses around me. There were very few people there so for the most part I had my choice of a large area. What I found interesting is how people would walk towards me then turn away when they reached the perimeter of the roses. They would walk around the perimeter instead of walking through my protected area. It was so much fun just to sit and watch.

You can protect your space at work too. Imagine roses at the doorway to your office or cubicle. If you are in an open area surround your desk with roses having them as high as you want them to be. The roses will act as a shield for your space. Observe how others respond.

ॐ

I love using this technique when I go to the movies.

Do you find that when you go to the movies someone tall sits in front of you? To create space around you at the movies imagine a rose in the seats you wish to be empty. I went to the movies one day and placed a rose in the seat in front of and one on each side of me. A woman and her mother sat down in front of me, which made me a little irritated. Much to my surprise within a minute they got up and left. No one replaced them so I had a clear view of the screen. Remember, keeping seats empty won't work at a sold out performance! Otherwise, enjoy the view.

(Also be aware of your beliefs. A friend of mine told me that whenever he went somewhere there was always a line in front of him. I told him it's funny because I'm always at the head of the line and then watch as others file in behind me. If you tell yourself that someone tall always blocks your view, then that will happen. Change your belief and use roses. The outcome will surprise you.)

Sending Love with Roses

Roses are beautiful, magical flowers that create a feeling of love when given or received. They bring warmth and beauty into a room. These flowers soften emotions in ways no one can explain. Imaginary roses are also magical and powerful when used in visualizations.

Tech. #43

Would you like to say "hello," "I love you" or "thank you" without picking up the phone or writing a note? Imagine a beautiful rose of any color. Bring the rose close to your heart. Next, visualize the words you want to say on an imaginary piece of paper, or see the words in the center of the rose. Put as much feeling as you can into the rose. Ask the rose to give your message to that special person, now visualize the rose leaving you and the recipient receiving the rose.

If the intended recipient is busy or distracted, he or she may not receive the message immediately. If it doesn't work right away, keep trying. It may take a few tries before someone realizes that they are getting a message from you. The thought might come through in the form of a warm feeling accompanied by an image of you, or it may actually be in the form of words. Or, you may have just popped into the recipient's thoughts. It's great to send love in any thought form and allow the universal energy to deliver it. This is a fun way to send a warm fuzzy to someone special.

Rebalancing Checklist

The rebalancing checklist is as follows:

- Sit with your feet on the floor, or lie down flat.
- Use any of the centering techniques. (Tech. 5, 6, 7)
- Summon all of your own energy back to yourself. (Tech. 13, 14)
- Release the energy of others from your body. (Tech. 19, 20, 21)
- Use any of the methods for running energy. (Tech. 10, 11, 12)
- Clear the chakras when necessary. (Tech. 22, 23, 24, 25)
- Protection (Tech. 35, 36, 37)

You don't need to go through each step every time. Nor is it necessary for you to find the time to sit down to use these techniques. Often times, you'll only have time to center yourself or to clear someone's energy out of your space or body. Use whatever you need at the time to help you feel comfortable. Occasionally take the time for yourself and use one technique per step. Help your body to relax and clear out the negative energies you've collected. You need to take care of your body and emotions by releasing others energy so you can deal with your issues and not theirs.

To feeling refreshed and healthier!

Chapter 6

BODY CHECKING

This technique has not been scientifically proven so use it at your own discretion. I have used it for various reasons and found it helpful.

Tech. #44

Kinesiology

Applied Kinesiology is the science of muscle testing. This determines the need for and effectiveness of treatment, as well as testing for food allergies, chemicals and other products. Chiropractors, Craniosacral Therapists, Touch for Health practitioners and other forms of non-typical western medicine providers use a form of this technique. The first technique teaches you how to test yourself and the second shows how to test with a partner.

Body Test Alone

Form a circle with the thumb and index finger of one hand. Press the two fingertips together firmly, but not to the point of straining. Put the index finger of your other hand through the circle touching the tip of the thumb on that hand. You will now have two circles interlocking with the fingertips held tightly together.

To body test, say to your body, "Body please give me a yes." Now try to pull the thumb-and-finger circles apart. Do your fingers part easily, or is there resistance? If the fingers remain interlocked then this is your body's "yes" response. However, if the circle breaks easily then that is your body's "yes" response.

Now link your fingers together again and ask, "Body please give me a no." Try to pull your fingers apart. This response should be the opposite of what you received for a yes. If your fingers stayed together for the "yes" then they should easily pull apart for the "no". You may have to repeat this exercise several times until you can distinguish clearly between the "yes" and "no" responses. Every time you use this technique you must test your body for its yes and no response. Your body may have switched because of something you ate or emotional stress.

If your body gives you reversed responses, that is, your fingers usually held together for yes and now your fingers come apart, then you will want to reset the responses. To set the responses back to normal, place your fingers on each side of your breastbone, about four inches below your collar bone. Rub the area with your fingers. Now re-test. You should now have returned to your normal yes/no response pattern. You have reset your body's response

Body Test With A Partner

Have your friend/partner hold his or her right or left arm straight out to the side or in front of them. Ask them to hold their arm as firm as they can. Now reach over and lightly push the arm down without hurting them. Does their arm hold in that position? It should. Have them either hold or taste some sugar. Now try pushing their arm down. Does the arm hold or collapse to their side? If their arm collapsed their body is telling them that sugar is not good for them. They loose physical strength when they have sugar. Test other foods to see how their body responds. Switch places and discover what foods or ingredients your body likes or dislikes.

Use the same method to test for yes and no responses. Hold your arm out. Have your partner say out loud, "Body, give me a yes". Have them try to push your arm down. Does it stay up or collapse down to your side? Then repeat asking for a no response. Does the arm stay up or collapse to your side? You should receive a different response for each question. Now you can use this technique to test foods, chemicals or questions about your body. Experiment!

❦

This type of body testing will also show you how negative thoughts affect your body. Repeat three times, "I am not a nice person." Have your partner push your arm down. What happened? Now repeat three times, "I am a wonderful person." Body test again, did your arm go down or did it stay up? If your arm went down on the negative and stayed up on the positive your body is telling you how important your thoughts are. Keep positive thoughts about yourself and your body will respond in kind.

❦

Very Important

If you body tested for physical disorders and something comes up that might imply a problem, do not rely on this technique. It is always important for you to consult your physician or health care provider. It isn't worth the risk. This technique should be used in situations that are not life threatening in any way.

The following are examples of body testing.

Does This Body Need_____?

Vitamins

First check your body for its "yes" and "no" response. To test whether or not you should take a certain vitamin and how much to take, place the container of the vitamin in question under your chin or arm. While holding the bottle mentally ask, "Does this body need [the name of the vitamin]?" If you get a "yes" response ask, "Does this body need one capsule?" If you got a yes then you're done, if you got a no then continue asking if the body needs two, three or more tablets or capsules? Now body check how many times per day to take the vitamins? (Check if this information is within range of the suggested dosage to avoid overdosing.)

Every day when it's time to take your vitamins, touch each bottle and ask out loud or mentally, "Does this body need vitamin [name] today?" and so on. If you get a "no" answer, skip it and go on to the next vitamin, repeating the question. Your need for vitamins varies according to your nutritional intake and energy output. You may have already satisfied your body's need for a particular vitamin and you don't want to overdose. Before I used this technique I used to take more iron and magnesium than I needed. My body let me know I had overdosed through my feet; they were very sensitive when I walked. Within a couple of days after I stopped taking the iron and magnesium my feet were no longer sensitive.

❧

Remember: Sometimes the body will reverse its "yes" and "no" response patterns. These patterns will reverse depending on your changes in dietary needs, stress, or other changes occurring in your life. You should re-evaluate your "yes" and "no" responses prior to each testing session. If the response is reversed, reset by rubbing each side of the breastbone.

❧

Here is an example of body testing with food. This is a little trickier because you must be precise with the phrasing of each question. For instance, if you seem to have problems with milk, you might ask, "Is this body allergic to milk?" and receive a "no" response. Rephrase the question by asking, "Can this body digest or assimilate milk." Perhaps you'll get a "no" answer again, indicating that even though you're not allergic to milk your body can't digest or assimilate it. This will confirm your feeling that milk isn't compatible with your body. Try using soymilk or rice dream as a substitute. Again, test your body for each item to discover which is best for you.

Here are some useful body checking questions:

"Does this body need [vitamin, vegetable, fruit, etc.]?"

"Is this body allergic to [name of item]?" (You can even ask if you're allergic to a particular person!)

"Can this body digest and assimilate [food item]?"

"Does this body need or require [a walk, exercise, dance, sleep, etc.]?"

"Does this body need or require a hug?" (You might need to give yourself a hug!)

"Would this body prefer decaffeinated coffee?"

"Is herb tea better for this body than coffee?"

"Does this body need or require rest?"

Note

Body testing is to assist you in better understanding your body and its needs. Maybe it will be an early detection system. Through body testing you might gain information that motivates you to seek a health care professional. *This is not a replacement for consulting a specialist in nutrition or any health care professional you might need.*

Listen to your body!

Finding Out Why

It's very important to pay close attention to your body, it's needs and what it's telling you. By combining body testing with paying close attention you will better understand or receive better insights to your body's needs. You know your body better than anyone.

Here's an example of how listening to my body and testing products helped me. When I was in my late thirties I began experiencing menopausal symptoms such as night sweats, moodiness, hair loss, and sleepless nights. Two doctors told me I was too young and couldn't be pre-menopausal. They were unwilling to help me with my symptoms. Finally, my moods were so bad and the night sweats so disturbing that I decided to go to the health food store. Hopefully I'd find something that would help. At first, I bought what was recommended without body testing. I still had trouble sleeping. A friend suggested that my body was probably getting too much estrogen. So, I took the product back and spoke to someone else about my symptoms. She suggested several new products. This time I tested each product and chose two. For the first time in years, I had a good night's sleep. Within three days, my moodiness subsided and I could tolerate myself. The night sweats greatly diminished and my hair stopped falling out. Body checking helped me to find products that suited my needs.

You can maintain a healthy body by listening to health care professionals and your body. Test your body against new products. Listen to your body.

(Do not use body testing for prescription medication. Please consult with your health care provider if you question the dosage or side affects.)

To a Healthy Life!

Chapter 7

MANIFESTING

People generally assume that the only way to attain personal objectives is through the application of goal-oriented strategies. But the unbelievable stress of trying to achieve what you want by employing strict living standards can be devastating. There is, however, another way to bring what you are wishing for into your life.

The process of manifesting can create results that would be difficult, if not impossible, to achieve through mere physical behavioral plans. We typically think that finding a desirable parking place or the perfect apartment or home is a matter of luck. No matter how effective your planning is, there is a point beyond which plans don't help and it seems that luck takes over. Manifesting, however, is more than luck. It is a method of encouraging the desired results to occur.

Manifesting is working with the universal energies. The universal energies include the help of God, The Divine, Great Spirit, Angels and Guides if you believe in these beings. It also includes your ancestors and friends who have passed. You've heard people say they felt that his or her mother, father, aunt or someone who passed was watching over them. They are and so are spiritual beings you didn't know personally. Universal energies give you access to these beings. Universal energies give you access to receive help from your community or from someone half way around the world. It's not necessary to know where the help is coming from or from whom, it will just appear. This is part of trusting what is to be.

Tech. #45

Four Simple Manifesting Rules

The four simple rules for manifesting are:
1. Make a clear decision of what you want.
2. List in detail the qualities that characterize your desire.
3. Make a clear image of yourself already enjoying what you want, remembering to give thanks for receiving what you've asked for or something better.
4. Let it go.

1.) Let's say you want to find a new place to live. You're tired of having a roommate, you want to leave your mate, or you feel a need to change your environment. Make a definite decision that you're ready to move. Be very clear that this is what you want. If you have any doubts—like maybe your roommate isn't really so bad, or maybe it's not the right time to leave your mate—you won't get what you want. Doubt automatically cancels an uncommitted wish. You must be very certain about your objectives.

2.) Next, make a specific listing of the qualities you desire in your new home. Do you want an apartment, duplex, cottage, or house? Do you want a studio or one or two bedrooms? Does the kitchen need to be large? Do you want carpeting or hardwood floors? Do you want a garage? How much can you afford to pay for rent or a mortgage?

Here's an example of how it works. (This was in the mid 1980's) I wanted to find a residence costing less than $800 per month, without a large deposit requirement, and in a quiet neighborhood north of San Francisco. I wanted two bedrooms, a large kitchen, hardwood floors, a fireplace, a garage, and a yard for my pets. My friends told me that it would be impossible to find such a place at that price. Well, I knew otherwise.

To my surprise, although I hadn't subscribed, the newspaper appeared daily on my doorstep. One Saturday morning I picked up the paper and, looked at the listings under "duplexes." (Until that day I had never looked under duplexes.) There it was. I knew instantly that I'd found my abode. I drove over immediately to look at my new home. Upon arriving, I looked in a window and saw an unappealing green shag carpet, vintage 1960s. Disappointed, I decided to investigate further. When the real estate agent arrived, he informed me that there were hardwood floors under the carpet, and he felt certain that the owners wouldn't mind removing the carpet. He was right. The duplex proved to have everything I was looking for and more. I moved in, my manifestation successful. I later manifested my Datsun 280ZX the same way.

3.) See or feel yourself in the new environment. Before you go to sleep or when you rise in the morning give thanks for your beautiful home or what ever you are manifesting. Always have gratitude for what you desire before and after you receive it. *Gratitude* is so important.

4.) The last step in manifesting can be a challenge. Once you've written down the qualities that you want it's time to *let go*. To help you in letting go, pretend that you hand the list of your desires over to someone else for safekeeping. You don't need to see it again; just put it out of your mind, *let it go*. Allow the universal energies to take over from here. Let them find and give you what you want. Now start looking for whatever it is you're seeking.

It's so important to *let it go*. If you hold on to your list too strong emotionally, you can prevent the desired result. It's as though you have that list clenched in your fist, holding it so tightly that the universe, God, and the Angels can't read what you've written. If they can't read it they can't give it. They can only give you what you want (or something better) when you let go. Let go and allow the universal energies to work with you. Together you can create a more peaceful and beautiful life.

Manifesting doesn't just apply to large ticket items like a home or car. You can manifest something as simple as a parking spot.

Nabbing Those Parking Spaces

Parking spaces are easy and fun to manifest. How close to your destination do you usually park? Are you always able to park within a block, right in front, or do you wind up four blocks away? Is your car scorching hot when you return? Why not park in front of your destination and when possible in the shade. Here's how.

Tech. #46

This is also considered working with the universal energies.

Make a mental statement that you want a parking place in front of your destination. Visualize the space. When you first begin to manifest parking spaces, you might have to go around the block once or twice. You either forgot to ask for one or you have doubts that you'll really find one. Trust that it will work. At some point you'll no longer need to ask, your space will be there when and where you want it.

I taught this technique to my husband and he always gets a space close to the door. It often makes me laugh.

Parking spaces are easy for me to manifest. One day, as I got into my hot car, I wondered why I hadn't been manifesting a shaded parking space. Now, whenever possible, I have a space in the shade. Due to the lack of trees on some streets I often settle for a space a block away but still close.

When manifesting, something like a parking space, allow your intuition, gut instinct, to guide you. Let your intuition determine the direction from which you enter the designated area. Have you ever reached your destination and across the street there's a parking space? When you follow your intuition you will approach the designated area from the correct direction and you'll find a space waiting for you. Practice manifesting parking spaces then see what else comes your way.

My friend Sue was always amazed at the ease with which I found parking spaces. One day she decided to manifest her own special parking place. Because she disliked having to maneuver backwards out of spaces, she wanted one that permitted her to drive straight through. Arriving at her bank, she found a space right in front, but to her dismay, there was a car in the space just ahead of it. Feeling slightly upset, she parked and proceeded into the bank. When she returned to her car, she was happily surprised to see that the car in front of hers was gone. She was able to drive straight through. The universal energies worked with her. Even though Sue didn't find the ideal parking space when she arrived, the ideal situation had materialized by the time she was ready to leave.

Remember to let go of the outcome of your manifestation. Do not become *attached* to the outcome you desire. The universe will often bring you something better. The more you practice manifesting the easier it will become.

Just as you no longer need to think in terms of goals, there will come a time when you no longer need to manifest your desires in life. When you begin living your life in trust, and following your inner guidance moment by moment, you will allow the universal abundance to come to you.... perfectly, as it should be.

Summary of Important Tips to Remember

1. Always do that which is for your highest good.

2. Ask for guiding help from God, The Divine, Great Spirit, your Higher Self/Spirit, Universe, Guides, Angels, or whomever or what ever you believe in. You will receive help, although not necessarily on your time schedule or in the manner you imagined.

3. Bring God's love, light, and healing energy into your heart, and be filled with its warmth. Always act from your heart.

4. Thank the Higher Power for all you have received, even if you have only five cents to your name.

5. Explore flower essences formulas. They're better than drugs to relieve many types of emotional distress.

6. Get a massage, go dancing (even if it's only at home), and walk in the forest or at the beach. Move your body as much as possible to help free blocked energy that may be stuck in various parts.

7. When receiving body or energy work, be sure to choose someone with whom you feel safe and comfortable. Body workers can put their negative energy and issues into your body, even without meaning to. If you feel uncomfortable, depressed, or tired after a session, ask yourself, "Is this my stuff or theirs?" If the answers is "theirs" clear the energy, and find someone else to help you.

8. Work in the yard, in the garden, or with houseplants. Connecting with Mother Earth is very healing.

9. Hum or sing a merry tune.

Chapter 8

SMILE AND RELAX

I t is often difficult to relax and enjoy life when you are surrounded by stressful situations. Whether its work, children, a dissatisfying relationship, or finances, stress can keep you unbalanced. If you don't have time to use all or some of the techniques already mentioned, the following will help your body instantly feel more relaxed and, hopefully, keep a smile on your face.

Easy Relaxation Exercises

The following are easy and quick ways to help you relax. When you feel stress whether you're at work, home, shopping or wherever, take a moment to calm yourself. Allow yourself time to stretch the muscles that have become tense. As you stretch these muscles take deep breaths. Inhale through your nose and fill your abdomen first and then your chest. Exhale through your mouth releasing the air from your abdomen first and then your chest. Through relaxing these muscles and breathing you will become more productive in your endeavors. These techniques take only a moment but will benefit you greatly. You can use these stretches in a series all at once or one or two at a time. Practice these techniques at home so when you need them you'll remember how to use them.

Tech. #47

Over Your Shoulder

Slowly turn your head to the right so your chin is over your right shoulder. Keep your chin up. Hold to the count of ten. Now turn your head to the left, keeping your chin up and over your left shoulder and hold to the count of ten. Turn your head back to the right then left. Repeat this exercise a minimum of five times. If you are feeling really stressed continue doing the exercise until you feel the muscles in your neck and face relax.

Breath!

Tech. #48

Side to Side

While facing straight ahead, allow your head to slowly drop to the side towards your right shoulder. Do not force your head to touch your shoulder and do not bring your shoulder up to touch your head. Feel the neck muscles on your left side stretch. Now, still facing ahead, bring your head straight up and allow it to slowly drop towards your left shoulder. Again, do not try to touch your shoulder or bring your shoulder up to your head. Feel the muscles on the right side of your neck stretch. This stretching will help the muscles along the sides of your neck relax. Repeat this technique ten or more times.

Breath!

Tech. #49

Front to Back

Looking straight ahead, slowly drop your chin to your chest to the count of four or longer if you desire. As you drop your chin to your chest you'll feel the muscles in your back being stretched. You'll begin to feel them relax and release the stress you've been holding. Now bring your head up to the count of four, and allow your head to fall slowly backwards toward your back to the count of four. At this point you will be looking at the ceiling. It's as though you are slowly nodding your head yes. Allow your head to go back as far as it is comfortable, but don't go to the point where you are straining to lift your head up again. As you look towards the ceiling you will find that your body will automatically take a deep breath. Take that deep breath and exhale as you lift your head. Slowly lift your head up to the count of four. Repeat ten times or as many times as needed to fully relax.

Breath!

Tech. #50

Neck Rotation

Make a circle with your head, beginning at your chest and ending at your chest. To the count of eight, drop you head to your chest and slowly rotate your head in a circle toward your left shoulder. Then rotate to the back as far as is comfortable, continuing toward your right shoulder and ending up at your chest. Repeat several times then switch directions. This will help your neck muscles and you will automatically begin taking deep breaths. Your whole body will begin to relax.

Tech. #51

Shoulder Lifts

Lift both your shoulders at the same time and slowly raise them towards your head. Just imagine yourself looking at your parents or boss. It's as though you are going to shrug your shoulders and say, "I don't know". As you slowly raise your shoulders, inhale. As you slowly drop your shoulders, exhale. This technique will get the energy flowing from your neck down through your torso. Repeat as often as needed or you desire.

Tech. #52

Shoulder Squeeze

Have someone stand behind you placing his or her hands on your shoulders at the neck with his thumb on your back and his fingers resting on your clavicle (collar bone). As he slowly applies pressure by squeezing the shoulder muscle he will bring the thumb and fingers towards each other moving the hands in an upward motion. It's as though your shoulders are being pinched and the tension is being pulled out of your body with the upward hand motion. As he brings his hands upward he needs to apply a little more pressure but not enough to make it uncomfortable. As your muscle is being squeezed, take a deep inhaling breath. As the muscle is being released, exhale. Repeat four times.

If your shoulders are really tense this may feel uncomfortable on the first two squeezes. You may need more than four squeezes to fully relax.

Afterwards the person who performed the shoulder squeeze should rinse their hands and wrist in warm or cool water. This will eliminate any energy they may have collected in their hands while helping you relax.

Tech. #53

Neck Release

Place your right pointer finger near the base of the neck, half way between the front of your neck and the side. Just above the clavicle (collar bone) you'll find a little hollow spot. From the hollow spot, move your finger up towards your head. Stop half way up the neck and move your finger gently back and forth. You should feel a band like ridge. To perform the neck release you'll move your finger gently towards the backside of the ridge. Apply pressure and move the finger forward to its original position. As you do this you should feel the ridge spring like a rubber band. Now, do the same on the right side using the left pointer finger. Don't be surprised if you feel a jolt of energy.

Next, go to the back of your neck. There is another ridge that runs parallel on each side of the spine. Place your finger on top of the ridge and move the finger towards the spine. Apply pressure inwards. When your finger is next to the spine bring the finger back towards the outside of the neck. You should feel the ridge pop back. Repeat on the opposite side.

This technique will bring a rush of energy throughout your head, especially if you're under a lot of tension. You can do this on others or have someone do this technique on you.

Dealing with Insomnia

When you find it hard to fall asleep at night, instead of counting sheep, try one or more of the following techniques.

Tech. #54

Hand Over Head

This is a technique you can use on yourself, partner or children to help them sleep. Use an open hand with the palm approximately three inches above the top of the head. If possible use your right hand. Hold your hand above the head for as long as possible. If you are helping someone else fall asleep you might be more comfortable if you lay next to them so your arm doesn't get tired. Or sit on the bed near enough so you aren't stretching you arm to reach the top of their head. It could take up to twenty minutes for the body to relax enough to fall asleep. (It probably won't take children long to fall asleep unless they are hyper from sugar or adrenaline. If they are, let them calm down before you use this method.) When you use this technique on yourself, notice how your body begins to relax from the head down. This technique has a very calming affect as it sends energy through the body.

Sleep in Divine Love and Light!

Tech. #55

Pull in Your Energy

Your energy field or aura extends out from your body. Have you ever noticed when a particular person walks into a room and the room seems to fill with their presence? You are feeling their energy field, aura, which extends several feet from their body. They might enjoy filling a room but at the same time they are bombarding everyone else and making them uncomfortable. When your aura expands several feet from your body it will pick up energy from those in the room. This may be why you can't get to sleep when you've returned home.

To help you sleep better you need to bring your energy in closer to your body. You might want to use clearing techniques as well. (Using the clearing techniques might put you to sleep too.) Pulling your energy field in is very simple. Say to your body. "Please bring my energy field to a distance of approximately 10 to 12 inches from my body." You can bring your aura in closer if you desire. This will calm the energy in your aura field.

To further assist you in sleeping, close your crown (7th) and throat (6th) chakras. These two chakras may be allowing too much energy into your body keeping your mind active. Too much energy flowing though your body will make you restless. Slow the energy down and sleep.

Sleep in comfort!

If you didn't clear the energy from your body before or after you entered your home then you will automatically dump it while you sleep. Your body will be in a relaxed state while you sleep allowing it to release much of the energy you accumulated. If you've never cleared the energy from your bedroom/mattress then you are sleeping in months of negative energy, most of which doesn't belong to you. If you have a partner, add the energy that they brought into the room. Think of the combined stressful energy from work, children and finances that both of you bring to the bedroom. You or both of you are trying to sleep in this negative energy. It's often difficult.

Tech. #56

Clear the Bedroom and Mattress

If you are having difficulty sleeping and you don't have a partner move to the other side of the bed. The other side of the bed should be clearer of any negative energy allowing you to sleep better. If you have a partner, move to the sofa or another bed if available for the night. Even though I clear the energy from our bedroom/mattress on a regular basis, I sometimes wind up sleeping elsewhere when my husband has had a stressful day. You might need to do the same.

As soon as possible, use the clearing techniques in the bedroom and on the mattress. To clear the mattress, place one or more coned shaped incense on something that can tolerate the heat (the cones get quite hot so use a glass ashtray or cup). Place the cones under the bed clearing the mattress from the bottom up. Or place the cones on top of the mattress. Be sure that the container can't tip or you'll have burn marks on the mattress. (I'm not sure if they can actually start a fire so be very careful.) For stick incense, place then in a container with salt, sugar or rice. Or hold them and wave them over the bed, as close to the mattress as possible. Clear the rest of the bedroom by placing additional incense throughout the room. This will help change the energy in the room allowing you to sleep better.

Clear the bedroom and mattress as often as possible or needed. Try to remember to clear the energy you accumulated during the day before you get home, especially before you go to bed.

Enjoy sleeping in peaceful energy!

Have you ever gone to bed and the same thoughts or ideas keep repeating or spinning through your mind? Maybe you are trying to compose a letter to someone you like or dislike. Are you making a mental list of all the things you need to do the next day, week or month? Is your mind in a constant state of chatter? The best way to stop the mind chatter is to write down the thoughts that are bombarding you. The reason you keep mulling things over in your mind is because you don't want forget them. A part of you thinks that if you go to sleep you'll forget everything. Often times you will but you don't need to.

Tech. #57

Write Your Thoughts

Keep a notepad and pen next to your bed. If you don't have a lot to write you may not need to turn the light on. If you have a lot to say or a long list, find a comfortable space and start writing. By writing everything down you can accomplish several goals.

First, your mind can relax and not worry that you'll forget something allowing you to fall asleep. Second, that long list of things to do will be done. All you'll need to do is refer to it and cross them off one by one. Third, if you're angry with someone you'll get those feelings out. There is nothing worse than holding onto anger and trying to sleep. Fourth, you might resolve the inner conflict you are having by discovering the core issue. It might take six pages of writing but let it flow. Because, once you discover the core of the issue you may not need to confront the individual and you will have gained some peace of mind.

The earlier you begin writing the faster you'll get to sleep.

Enjoy a peaceful nights rest!

Tech. #58

Give Thanks

Giving thanks is a great way to connect to God or the Divine. As you lie in bed and give thanks, ask God to fill you with love and appreciation. Then begin giving thanks by mentioning every single item you are grateful for. Give thanks for each of your children, your spouse, your family, your beautiful home (no matter what it looks like), your car whether it runs well or not, your pets, and your job. Give thanks for the friends you have lost or no longer see, the friends you now have and the friends yet to come into your life. Look back on your life and give thanks for all that you have been given, all that you currently have and all that you will have in the future. Be thankful for all the good things that have come into your life and all the lessons you have had along this incredible journey. Be thankful for the good and the bad. For all things have brought you to where you are today. Remember God gives all that benefits you, how you look at it is up to you. So be grateful for the broken down car or the large financial windfall. Both deserve your thanks.

Giving thanks enables you to step out of self-pity and into a place of gratitude. When you bring yourself into a position of gratitude you change your perspective. Gratitude will help you feel love not loss. Be thankful for everything in your life. Be content with where you are and what you have. Connect with the Source and feel love. And close with, "I love you God, and thank you for loving me."

Blessings!

Tech. #59

Give Yourself a Hug

Bring your energy into your heart. Imagine all your thoughts flowing from your mind down into your heart. Ask your heart to open. See or feel yourself in a place that's safe like a special room, the beach, the forest or anywhere that's special to you. This special place is located in your heart center. Ask that another part of you, no matter how old, join you. As you look at yourself notice how you appear. Are you happy, tired or sad? Walk over to that part of yourself and wrap your arms around him or her. Send love to them and say, "I love you". Hold yourself in your arms for as long as you desire. Mentally list all the wonderful attributes you have. Love yourself fully for you are a beautiful being of love.

Appreciate all that you are!

Tech. #60

Drinking Water and More

If you've had too much sugar, caffeine, alcohol, or heavy food, drink lots of water. Try to do this as early in the evening as you can. This should help you eliminate or flush through your body the toxins which keep you awake.

Over time I have found that the following also helps. These are suggestions of what has worked for me. Be sure you are comfortable taking them, *if you have doubts or problems that persist, consult your physician or health care provider.*

If you had alcohol during the evening, take vitamin B as it helps replenish the vitamin B that alcohol strips from your body.

If I have a soda a day for three consecutive days I have difficulty sleeping. Compared to most individuals, that isn't much. But if three sodas in three days keep me from sleeping it might be affecting you too. You might want to re-assess your intake. Some bodies are more sensitive to certain products than others. When my intake of sodas keeps me from sleeping I take Banlangen Tea. It's a Chinese tea that I discovered years ago. It seems to cleanse caffeine and sugar from my blood stream in a matter of minutes allowing me to fall asleep. (Google Banlangen Tea to find it on the web.) You can either make Banlangen into a drink or simply swallow the granules with water.

Drink other herbal teas like chamomile or you might enjoy warm milk to help you relax.

There are two other herbs that I have found of great value for me they are Milk Thistle and Valerian Root. Milk Thistle helps the liver process toxins such as sugar, caffeine and alcohol while Valerian Root helps the body relax.

Your stomach may be having trouble digesting the food you ate that evening. Take something for your stomach. Sometimes the stomach goes into a spasm and a simple aspirin will help it relax. Or you might need something like Pepto-Bismol or Maalox.

Pay attention when you have trouble sleeping, what have you eaten or had to drink that day? Your body may be having a difficult time assimilating certain foods and drinks. If you are under a lot of stress you might be ingesting more sugar or caffeine. Your body will tell you when something is wrong; sleep deprivation is one way the body will talk to you. Take care of the body and it will allow you to sleep better. The body can only handle so much. So be good to your body.

Sleep tight!

Tech. #61

Quit Trying

If you tried several techniques and still can't sleep, quit trying. The harder you try the more stress you place on your body. The more stress you experience the more exhausted you will become. Then it becomes impossible to fall asleep.

Transition is another reason you might not be able to sleep. If you've had some changes in your life your emotional, mental and physical body need to process those changes. When energy is shifting it's difficult for the body to sleep because the body is unable to process during the day. Working, teaching, cleaning, raising children, all keep your emotional, mental and physical body too active to allow a transition. The body needs to release old unwanted energy and receive new clear energy. When nightfall comes every thing slows down. Most people are asleep and the energy in your city slows down. That's why transition happens at night and keeps you awake. Allow the mind to wander, don't worry about sleeping and don't edit the thoughts. You might discover something wonderful.

When the mind wanders it is more receptive to information coming from God, The Divine, your inner Spirit or whomever. So listen with your heart, relax and allow your thoughts to be open. Go with the flow of what the night might bring. If you stay relaxed you will find that you won't feel tired or cranky in the morning even if you receive six or less hours of sleep. This happened to me and for five months I got approximately two to four hours of sleep each night. Because I stayed open and didn't get stressed about the lack of sleep, I didn't get irritable or exhausted. Once the transition passed I began sleeping six to eight hours.

Allow the process to take its course.

৯

If your body became stressed while trying to go to sleep, relax each part of your body separately. Begin with your feet then legs and move up the body. To relax your body begin by saying, "my feet are very relaxed and are going to sleep." Move up to your legs, "My right calf is very relaxed and going to sleep now the left calf is very relaxed and going to sleep." Pause between each body part to allow it to relax. Continue up your leg and relax the thighs. Now start on the body torso. Relax all the organs and muscles from you waist down. Move to the upper organs and muscles, neck, arms, head and mind. Mention as many body parts and organs as you can while relaxing them. You are hypnotizing your body to sleep. Hopefully you'll be asleep before you reach your head and mind.

Enjoy the process!

SLEEP WELL!!

Chapter 9

SIMPLE HEALING TECHNIQUES

These healing techniques are to help you feel better. They will help you relieve pain, help wounds heal faster, relieve tired eyes and pick up your energy. You can use them on yourself, partner, children, friends or anyone needing a little extra TLC. These techniques are not going to cure you from any illness. These techniques are **not** meant to turn you into a healer. They are to help **you** relieve your pain or help you relieve someone else's pain and feel more comfortable. *You should always see your health care provider for any injury or illness.*

Intent

Your *intent* is always important when using any healing technique. As long as you have a clear intention to help yourself or someone else feel or get better you are coming from your heart. It is also important that you do not become attached to how the healing process occurs or its outcome. With a positive attitude to assist as much as you can, the rest is up to the way things are meant to be.

When helping others it's important to understand that some people subconsciously don't really want to be helped. They are comfortable with being ill even if they say otherwise. For whatever the reason they unconsciously want to have health issues. In the same light, everyone has a path to walk in this life and illness may be part of their life's lessons. Never judge someone for their health issues and whether or not they get better. Do your best to help and the rest is up to them. Nor is it your responsibility to see that they are healed. Every one is responsible for the outcome of his or her own well-being. On the other hand, if both parties are willing, you can help others and yourself feel better.

༄

Important Note:

If you are helping someone else, perhaps someone who is or was in the hospital, it is important not to put your energy into his or her body. Clear any blocked energy from your arms and hands by using imaginary roses. Take an imaginary rose and run it down your arm, clearing the energy. Place the rose in an imaginary fire and retrieve another rose to clear the energy from your hand. Using a circular motion, clear the center of your palm and the fingers, then place the rose in the fire. You can also use your fingers to push the energy from the top of your arm down and out. Massage your hand and push the energy out through each fingertip. Pretend that you are squeezing the energy out of your body.

Once you've cleared the energy from your arms and hands, ask that God's (or higher power's) light, love, and healing energy enter through the top of your head. Ask the energy to continue down through your throat, split at the shoulders, and move down your arms and out through your fingertips. Then you will be ready to place your hands on someone else and help them. You never want to put your energy into someone else's body. Instead of helping them they will feel uncomfortable and not know why. Unless they too know these techniques they won't know that they have collected your energy in their body nor will they know how to eliminate the unwanted feelings this energy can cause.

Whenever you want to help others feel relaxed or help them clear energy from their body, be sure you are very familiar with the how to. You will be more aware of what is happening and when they tell you how they are feeling you will be able to relate. And remember, intent is always top priority when you help others. If you believe in a higher source then ask for guidance from that source.

Afterwards remember to run your hands and wrists under cool water to clear their energy.

Releasing Pain

If you, your mate, children, friends or pets get hurt, you can help *relieve their pain* (not cure them) and *speed up the healing process*. This technique will also help relieve the pain of menstrual cramps, some headaches, gaseous stomachs, toothaches, and many types of injuries. Should your child get injured, degree of severity doesn't matter, use this technique, they will love you for it. If someone's had surgery, including dental work, this will help relieve the pain as well as help him or her heal. The length of time you need to apply the technique is determined by the severity of the pain.

Helping Others

To be of better service to someone, after a major injury or surgery, you might prepare yourself by first going within your heart for a short period of silence. You can say a prayer and ask for guidance so you can better help them. If you wish, ask that you be surrounded with love, light and healing energy. Before you begin working on someone it's important for you to make a connection with him or her. Place your hands on his or her arms, leg, feet, hands or whatever is comfortable for them. This will enable you to connect on an energetic level. Once you've made the connection you can begin working.

Here's an example of how **pain drain**, Tech. # 62 can help you or someone else. My boss slammed her thumb in a car door. She told me her thumb was flat when the door was finally opened. Because I was able to work on her immediately after the accident her fingernail did not turn black or fall off. The only pain she felt was when she applied pressure on the bone.

When the body no longer needs to release the initial impact of the injury it can focus on the healing that it needs to do. The body has steps it needs to take to heal an injury. When the injury first occurs the body has the initial pain or trauma to address. Once that is over it can heal the injured tissue. When the initial pain or trauma is released immediately it relieves the body from having to take those steps. Instead it can immediately address the injured tissue and start making its repairs. You can test this without having an injury. After a dental appointment, use **pain drain** to relieve the affects of the Novocain. You will find that the pain will be released and the Novocain will dissipate from your body quickly. But, don't hesitate to use this technique on you or someone else should the need arise.

Intent is very important. Even though you may not know how this works, trust that it will and that you or the individual will feel better.

Tech. #62

Pain Drain

When doing healing work, the flow of energy is from the left to the right. The left hand will receive the energy and the right hand will release it.

Place your left palm over the injured area. The left palm will act as a vacuum and pull the painful energy up into your hand. Imagine the energy flowing up your left arm, straight across your shoulder, down your right arm and emptying out through your right palm. Place your right palm face up towards the sky to allow the energy to flow away from your body. Ask the universe to transmute the energy to a higher form. (You can also imagine the energy flowing into a fire to be transmuted.)

It is very important that you do not have the energy flow into the rest of your body. For example, as the energy flows from your left arm to your right, do not have the energy flow into your body or head. Keep it flowing directly across the body from one shoulder to the other and down the right arm. You may feel the energy clear or you can ask the person you're working on to tell you when the pain has subsided.

To clear the energy from your hand and body point the palm of your left hand toward the sky. Ask that healing energy flow into your left hand, up your arm, across the shoulders and down the right arm leaving through the right palm. Allow the healing energy to flow through this path for a minute or two. This will clear the injured energy from your body.

Next, you will want to place healing energy into the injured area. Keep your left hand, palm up, facing the sky. Place your right hand on the injury. Ask for healing energy to flow through your left hand to the right hand. Use the same path as you did when you removed the painful energy. Continue to let healing energy flow into the injured area for two to three minutes, longer if you wish.

You may need to use this technique more than once or twice on the same injury. If it's a small scratch once will do but if it's a bad cut or surgery you will need to repeat several times. Use your discretion or the desire of the individual you are working on.

᠊ᢙᢙ᠊

Here's another example: A friend of mine fell, cutting her leg. She had 27 stitches and because the cut was so deep, the doctor thought she would need skin grafts. I worked on her leg the same day as the injury, which can made a difference in the healing process. Due to the severity of the injury I worked on her leg three or four different times. After the first healing session, she went back to the doctor, who was amazed at how fast her leg was healing. After the third healing session, the doctor was further amazed, you had to look hard to see if there was a scar.

Don't feel you have to make the pain go completely away or heal the injury. Not every one's body will heal the same. If someone has diabetes they will not heal as well as someone without diabetes. If you use this technique on someone and they were told by their doctor to rest but instead they play golf, the healing won't be as affective. Do your best and allow the universe to take care of the rest. Don't get caught up in whether or not you did a good job. The amount of healing a person is willing to receive is up to them. Your intent is to help them relieve pain not cure them.

Allow it to be!

Relieving Distress in the Body

Tech. #63

Stomachache

You can use this technique on anyone, including your pets.

Have the person sit or lie down. If you are working on a child, place the children on their stomach. For a pet, hold them in your arms, or for a large pet sit beside them. Place your thumb gently alongside the spine. Slowly move your thumb down the spine from the shoulders to the hips. The area that is most affected is approximately two to four inches above the waist. You will either feel or hear intestinal gas, like air bubbles. If you feel an area that is hard, hold your thumb on the spot for a while, gently pressing. It can take a few minutes until the gas begins to move. You may have to work this area for five minutes, depending on the amount of gas accumulated.

You may not clear the gas out completely, but the pain should be relieved enough to make a person or animal feel comfortable. When my animals can't settle down to sleep, I put my ear to their stomachs. If it's really gurgling, I use this technique and in a few minutes they settle down.

There are a lot of remedies for hiccups. This is the one remedy that I have found that works at least 90% of the time if not more. Hiccups are the spasmodic contraction of the diaphragm. This remedy works directly with the nerves in the spine and the diaphragm.

Tech. #64

Hiccups

From the base of the neck, where the neck meets the back of your skull, count three vertebrae down (third cervical). You might have to apply pressure in different spots if you can't find the third cervical right away. Eventually you'll find the right spot. The third cervical is the origin of the nerve that leads to the diaphragm. Gently apply pressure alongside the vertebra until the hiccups stop. The pressure you apply will help relax the spasm and stop the hiccups. You can use this technique on adults and children. It may be a little more difficult to find the right spot on babies because their necks are so short, children will be much easier.

Another technique to help relieve hiccups:

Place the thumb and pointer finger of one hand together. This creates energy flowing like a laser. To test, point the two fingers at the palm of your other hand. Move them around to see if you can feel the energy. Point your fingers approximately four inches below the sternum (breast bone) in the center of your body. This distance will be less on an infant or child. You will be pointing the laser at the diaphragm. This will help the diaphragm to relax.

Another way to locate this point is to gently feel the ribs, which come from the sternum, slightly moving outward. From the spot where the lowest rib connects to the center of the body, move your fingers down several inches. Continue to point at this spot until the hiccups stop. If they don't stop, you may have to search until you find the exact spot of their origin.

You can also use the laser affect if you have a toothache, headache or other physical pain. Do a figure eight movement over the area several times. Imagine the pain attaching itself to the laser and pull the laser away from your body. It will seem as though you are pulling a string from your body. Place the pain in a bowl and burn it.

On a daily basis you probably do a fair amount of computer work, construction or other work that can make your eyes feel tired or irritated. The computer screen and glare put a considerable amount of stress on eyes. If you work outdoors your eyes are exposed to pollution and the elements. All are harmful to your eyes and add to the stress of your body. Here is a simple technique that will help relax your eyes.

Tech. #65

Tired or Irritated Eyes

One of the most vulnerable spots in the body is the eye. This is a simple technique to help relieve the stress the eyes are feeling. (If there is any damage to the eye, see a physician immediately. You don't want to risk loosing your sight.)

Relieve the tiredness or irritation to one eye at a time. Use one or more imaginary roses. Visualize the petals of the rose partially opened. Then imagine the petals going through the front of the eye. Slowly move the rose deeper into the eye until it reaches behind the eye. You may need to imagine the rose reaching into the optic nerve. As the rose enters the eye, it will pick up energy from any stress or irritation the eye is feeling. The degree to which your eyes feel tired will determine the number of times you'll need to repeat the process. As you pull each rose out, place it in an imaginary fire. This allows the energy to be released and transmuted. Repeat the process for the other eye.

You can actively participate in the visualization. You can pretend that you are going through the motions. Reach out your hand and pick a rose from the universe. Now slowly insert the imaginary rose into your eye. Move the rose slowly all the way to the back of the eye. Slowly pull the rose out and place it into a fire.

(Also see Releasing and Replacing Pain.)

Energy Pick Me Ups

Energy is emitted outwards from everyone's body. This energy creates an aura. The aura can extend from a few inches to several feet away from the body. If you have heard the expressions, "you are in my space" or "you're invading my territory," it refers to one's aura. When you are the only one in an elevator do you step back when someone else gets on? If so, you are feeling someone entering your aura. You feel uncomfortable. To help you feel more comfortable, you can adjust the distance your aura expands from your body. Ask your aura to come within twelve or less inches from your body. The first couple of times you do this, you may feel uncomfortable almost claustrophobic, but you'll get used to it. You, like most people, are used to having your aura extended far from your body, not close in. That's why you will feel an invasion of your space when someone gets near. By drawing your aura in and adding protection you won't feel invaded.

You can call your aura in any time or any place. It is really as simple as saying, "I ask that my aura come in twelve inches, or closer (if you desire), from my body." If you keep your aura drawn closer to your body you won't need to clean others energy out as often. But if you feel like you need a fun pick-me-up the following two techniques will help.

This may seem like a strange technique but it really works. It is actually easier if you have someone else fluff your aura and you do his or hers. But, if you need to do it yourself you will fluff enough of your aura to make you feel better.

Tech. #66

Fluffing the Aura

Standing approximately two feet away from a person, you will fluff the aura from the ground up. Begin with your hands, palm up, on the floor. Slowly, while alternating between hands, direct each hand upward in a steady motion. Move your hands six to eight inches at a time. Move from the floor to the top of the head. Then return to the floor, rotating a step to your right or left. Continue around the body and return to the starting point. Now have them fluff your aura.

When you work on yourself, have your arms extended and your elbows close to your body. With palms facing towards your body, begin at your feet and move upwards. Slowly stand up as you move your hands in the upward motion. Continue until you are standing upright and finish with your hands slightly over your head. You will move in a circle using the intent that when you are finished, you will have fluffed the aura around your entire body.

Notice the difference in how you feel whether you fluff your own aura or have someone do it for you. The energy around your body will feel more relaxed almost restful. Test it on your children or partner and see what affect it has on them.

The following process is similar to aura fluffing but goes deeper with shifting the energy to a lighter state. This is a visualization for cleansing your body. If you have a partner, have him or her follow the same format. This is another great way to fall asleep while doing a final cleansing for the day.

Tech. #67

Body Cleansing or Raking

While lying down imagine your fingers slightly apart with your thumbs touching. Your hands will be approximately two to three inches above the body. Point your fingers towards the body and begin five or six inches above the top of the head. Imagine your hands moving slowly towards your feet. Your hands and the movement will remind you of raking leaves. You will be raking the energy from above your head, through your body and out past your feet. The rake, your fingers, will accumulate the negative energy just like a garden rake accumulates leaves. When you get to the feet, continue moving your hands as though you are tossing leaves into a pile. Toss the energy into a pile, moving the energy away from the body.

Continue this movement ten to fifteen times down the center of the body. Repeat the technique down the left side, then the right side. Rake all three positions ten to fifteen times. This will ensure you're clearing the body and aura as well.

You can either push the energy into an imaginary fire each time you make the raking movement down the body or place the energy in a pile and burn it at the end of the session.

You can clear someone else's body by doing the same movements. Instead of using your imagination you will actually be moving your fingers above their body.

❧

Here's a variation on the same technique.

Lie down and get comfortable. You might want to turn on meditation or relaxation music. Visualize a wide rake that covers the width of your body and extends at least a foot on each side. Have the rake approximately two to six inches above your body. Begin the raking movement eight inches above your head. Have the prongs of the rake slowly flow through your body picking up any excess energy that does not belong to you. Bring the rake down the entire length of your body and continue below your feet. Rake the excess energy into an imaginary fire. Repeat this as often as you need to clear your energy or until you fall asleep.

Enjoy the feeling!

Chapter 10

MEDITATION

Webster's definition of *meditate* is "to reflect upon; study; ponder or to think deeply and continuously." My definition includes "to quiet the mind, to listen to God, The Divine, Great Spirit or whoever you believe in". Meditating is a form of allowing your mind to receive or to listen to The Divine. Meditating should not be confused with praying. Praying is telling the Divine what you are thankful for and want. Praying doesn't require you to quiet the mind like meditating does. Quieting the mind takes practice.

There are many forms of meditation. You can attend classes and workshops that teach a number of traditional approaches. If you haven't yet had the time, money, or inclination to take classes or workshops, the following simple techniques will help you begin. They can be used if you have a moment or two before you fall asleep, awaken a few minutes early, or have quiet time during the day. Depending on your time and emotional state, use different techniques at various times. For example, your fears can interrupt your communication with God and won't allow you to be open enough to receive clear answers. In this case you might want to use the **chakra opening** technique because it will take you into a deeper meditative state.

To meditate you can either lie down or sit with your legs crossed. The generally accepted position is sitting with your legs crossed. This position allows the energy to flow better. For me, when I sit I need to have my head rest against the back of the chair or it bobs and scares me. Of course, I've probably fallen asleep, which is common. My favorite posture while meditating is to lie down. That way if I fall asleep I'm in a comfortable position although I don't believe that's what you are supposed to do. Use whatever position works best for you. When you first begin to meditate you may find that you fall asleep too. That's okay. Eventually, you will find you stay awake. Once you've tried each meditation you may find that you like one or two the best. Use the one(s) that work best for you.

To assist you in meditating, you might want to try listening to a relaxing meditation cd. Meditation music will help distract the mind from chatter. The music gives the mind something to focus on. There are a wide variety of meditation cds available: Steven Halpern has several, a few of them are *Inner Peace, Music for Healing* and *Chakra Suite*; three of Riley Lee's are *Sanctuary, Music for Zen Garden, Music for Zen Meditation* and *Satori*; two of Nawang Kchechog's cds are titled *Tibetan Meditation Music* and *For Quiet Mind & Peaceful Heart*; and Aine Minogue's *Celtic Meditation Music*.

Tech. #68

Hand to Heart

This is a very easy way for you to relax and enter a meditative state. Lie down in a comfortable position. Place your left hand over your heart, and then place your right hand on top of the left hand. As you lie there you will gradually relax. You will feel yourself go through different stages of relaxation. Eventually, your mind will stop thinking of all the things you should be doing and your body will feel lighter. The more you use this technique, the less time it will take you to relax and let go. When you quiet your mind, you will have other thoughts enter. Instead of thinking of what needs to be done, you will receive thoughts that will guide you on or through your life's path and direction. You may receive insight to questions or problems you are trying to resolve. Pay attention to those thoughts because they are coming from The Divine or your Higher Self/Spirit.

You can add healing energy to this technique if you wish. If you do, be sure to run the energy through your body for a minute to clear any old, blocked energy.

Here's To New Insights!

Tech. #69

Opening the Chakras

If you are new to meditation, it may take time before you notice your mind quieting enough to reach a true state of peace and calm. This is a powerful meditation technique. You'll love the feeling.

The following meditation includes the seven chakras, the high heart, the 8th chakra located above your head, and your knees and ankles. To "open" the chakras, move in a circle from left to right. Upon concluding the meditation, you will close the chakras by moving in the opposite direction, in a circle from right to the left. It's a good idea to practice the technique several times before meditating so that it becomes a natural process.

You will begin and end at the heart (4th) chakra. Hold each point for two minutes or more. Find a quiet comfortable place to lie down. Add meditation music if you desire as it might help. Place one hand on top of the other for all the positions except the knees and ankles.

1. Begin by placing both hands over your heart (4th) chakra and hold.
2. Moving your hands towards the left side of your body, bring your hands in a semi-circle down to rest on the naval (3rd) chakra.
3. Moving your hands towards the right side of the body, bring your hands in a semi-circle up to your high heart (between your heart and throat).

Continue making half circles to each new position.

4. Moving towards the left, bring your hands to the 2nd chakra, two inches above your pelvic bone.

5. Moving towards the right, bring your hands to the throat (5th) chakra.
6. Moving towards the left, bring your hands to the 1st chakra. If you can, place your hands between your legs palms facing towards your body. If your arms are not long enough, place your hands on the pubic bone.
7. Moving towards the right, bring your hands to your forehead (6th) chakra.
8. Moving towards the left, with your hands apart, point the palms of each hand towards each knee.
9. Moving towards the right, place your hands (now back together) on the top of your head (7th) chakra.
10. Moving towards the left, with your hands apart, point the palm of each hand towards a foot, right hand to right foot and left hand to left foot.
11. Moving towards the right, point the palms of your hands (now together) up above your head towards the 8th chakra (approximately six to eight inches above your head).

Once you have finished opening the chakras stay in this meditative state for as long as you wish. Don't worry if you fall asleep when you first start to use this technique. When you are finished or wake up do not forget to close the chakras. If you do forget you might feel unbalanced and unsteady. You are also leaving yourself wide open for the interference of other's energies. Not closing the chakras will also leave you off center and could leave you open for an accident whether it's a fall or in your car.

Closing is the reverse of the opening. Your hands will be just as they were in opening the chakras.

To close: hold each point five to ten seconds.

1. Begin with the 8th chakra. Hands pointing upward towards the 8th chakra.
2. Moving to the right, point your hands towards your feet.
3. Moving to the left, place hands on the top of your head (7th).

4. Moving to the right, point your hands towards your knees.
5. Moving to the left, place hands on your 6th chakra.
6. Moving to the right, place your hands on the 1st chakra.
7. Moving to the left, place your hands on your 5th chakra.
8. Moving to the right, place your hands on the 2nd chakra.
9. Moving to the left, place your hands on the high heart.
10. Moving to the right, place your hands on the 3rd chakra.
11. Moving to the left, place your hands on your 4th chakra, your heart. You are back to where you began and have completed the closing of the chakras.

Take a few moments before you get up and move around. Allow the energy and the feeling to fully saturate your body, heart and soul. Enjoy the expansion of your soul and who you are.

In Peace and Love!

Tech. #70

Walking or Sitting

A great way to meditate, and a favorite of mine, is to hike in the woods, or to sit on a beach or by a stream or river. (Nature is my church.) The mind will quickly clear allowing you to bring in your Higher Self or The Divine. You will find that the ocean or any body of water will help clear your energy due to the negative ions. Try to be alone during this time. If you need to have a partner with you for safety reasons don't walk side by side or sit next to each other. Allow some space between you so your energies won't blend. Do your best not to talk

When there are no outside distractions, you can experience a profound stillness of your mind. You will also begin to see your surroundings more vividly and clearly, feeling at one with all you encounter. When you meditate in nature you will begin to connect to the energy of nature and what it provides for you. You will appreciate your surroundings more, leaving yourself open to perhaps see that which does not have physical forms. There's a lot that goes on in nature that you might not be aware exists.

If you are in the forest, become part of the trees and foliage. Be aware of the energy in your surroundings. Feel the universal forces of nature and embrace it, as you are a part of it. Energy flows through you and everything around you. Become one with nature. Feel Mother Earth's energy flow into your feet and up your body as you slowly and silently walk upon her elegance. If you are near water, focus your mind on the water and become one with it. If you can, become part of the waves coming to shore. Enjoy the calming affect that the negative ions have on your body.

Enjoy the beauty around you and you will enjoy the beauty within!

Tech. #71

Thumb and Finger (Mudras)

This technique is used in many meditation practices. One day I decided to try it and was amazed at how quickly the energy began flowing evenly and peacefully through the center of my body. My mind quieted within a short period of time. I entered the meditative state without much struggle on my part. This is a lovely technique to use while in bed before going to sleep as well as when sitting in a chair getting ready to receive answers from a Higher Source.

This technique is known as the Gyan Mudra. My knowledge of the Gyan Mudra is limited so I am relying on information obtained from a friend. Instead of doing this on your own, you may choose to find a teacher of Gyan Mudra.

The following are five different ways to meditate using Gyan Mudra. While using any one of these meditations you might want to play some nice meditation music and get comfortable.

The first is known as the basic and most commonly used Mudra, which stimulates knowledge and wisdom. It also helps with creating receptivity and calmness. Place the tip of your index (pointer) finger with the tip of your thumb to form a circle.

The second is considered the more "active" form of the basic. Instead of having the finger tips touch, place the fingernail of your index finger against the back of the thumb. Just slide the finger under the thumb and hold.

The third position is called the Shuni Mudras. The Shuni Mudra helps give you patience, commitment, as well as discernment. With the Shuni Mundra you place the tips of your middle finger to the tip of your thumb again forming a circle. If you are coping with issues related to karma this would be a good position to use. The middle finger is associated with Saturn which deals with the laws of Karma.

The fourth finger position is called the Surya Mudra. This position is great for revitalizing energy, good health and the nervous system. You will use your ring finger which is associated with the Sun and Uranus. The Sun deals with energy, health as well as sexuality. On the other hand, Uranus is associated with the nervous system and intuition. To form this mudra, place the tip of your ring finger to the tip of your thumb forming a circle.

The fifth finger position deals with mental clarity and is called Buddhi Mudra. Using the Buddhi Mudra will help enhance your ability to communicate clearly, enhance your intuition and stimulate psychic development. Place the tip of your little finger to the tip of your thumb forming a circle. When using the little finger you connect to Mercury which helps your mental power.

With each of these positions have your palms facing upwards and resting on your legs or by your side. Concentrate on the music to keep your mind from making lists or rehashing the day. Flow with the music and allow yourself to be taken away on a cloud or just float through the universe enjoying everything you see and feel. Ask for the company of angels or maybe a relative or friend who is on the other side to join you. This gives you a wonderful opportunity to talk and reconnect with someone who has passed even if you only want to say, "I love and miss you". Go with and be in the moment.

Enjoy your meditation!

IN CLOSING

I hope you enjoy becoming familiar and working with energy using the techniques I have described for you. Since energy is in everything and everyone, it's important to learn what it is and how to work with it. There's nothing mysterious about energy, it's just a matter of becoming conscious of how to use it in a positive way. The more you use these techniques the easier they will be and, soon, they will become second nature to you. You will work with energy without thinking about it and have a better understanding of the universal forces.

But it's not only important for you to work with energy. There are more children coming onto this planet that have intuitive gifts and need to learn these techniques so they can better protect themselves. I had the honor of working with a three year old that could see colors, spirits and other visions beyond our five normal senses. The problem was his mother didn't know what to say to him to help him understand what he was seeing and feeling. Once he understood he was less frightened.

Watch different children in public places. Some are so sensitive to energy that it's uncomfortable for them to be where there are large groups of people. For others, they might stare at you and smile. If you are fortunate to have one or more of these children, please understand that they need to know how to protect themselves and their energy. In today's world, even if they don't have intuitive gifts, children need to know how to protect themselves from others. So, I highly recommend that you teach your children as many techniques as you can. Help them be more comfortable in their bodies and their surroundings.

In The Divine's Love and Light

Blessings to You

ABOUT THE AUTHOR

Judy May
Intuitive Spiritual Counselor/Healer

I consciously began working with energy in the early 1980's. I took psychic development classes and later worked with intuits to begin my own healing process. Later, I expanded and simplified these techniques while using them on myself: These are the same techniques I use with clients and teach in my books *HEALING YOUR HEART and 71FUN WAYS*.

I have found a wonderful sense of inner peace using the techniques in my books. It has been a long, yet short, journey to where I am and the amazing thing is, it continues to get better every day. We all receive compassion and understanding as we heal our pain. That is what I have found and want others to experience and gain. I feel that we will only achieve world peace when we, as a whole, have inner peace. There are many wonderful people, such as Oprah and now Dr. Phil, helping this transition. My books can be of assistance too.

While working with clients I am able to see, hear and feel the answers and issues they are dealing with. This enables me to help them reach deeper and discover the core of the issue not just deal with the peripheral issue. I teach and direct my clients to heal within their heart center. For most individuals being in their heart center is uncomfortable but with time they are able to stay focused within their heart to heal at a deeper level.

Two of the most important healing factors are for individuals to reclaim their soul and to unite with their spirit and God or Higher Source. The goal is to live as a Spiritual Being with love and compassion.

Please feel free to e-mail me at jkmay50@yahoo.com

Live in The Divine's Love & Light

Blessings

OTHER SOURCES

Louise L. Hay, *You Can Heal Your Life* Hay House

Barbara Ann Brennan. 1987. *Hands of Light: A Guide to Healing Through theHuman Energy Field.* New York: Bantam Books.

Healing Touch Workshops. Lakewood, CO. (303) 989-0581 Janet Mentgen.

Bowen Hands Workshops. Victoria, Australia. Oswald and Elaine Rentsch. (03) 5572-3000.

877580

Made in the USA